The Story of Zhuang Zi

Written by Zhang Fuxin
Translated by Zhang Tingquan

Foreign Languages Press   Beijing

First Edition   2002
Second Printing 2003

Managing Editor: Liang Liangxing

Home Page:
    http://www.flp.com.cn
E-mail Addresses:
    info@flp.com.cn
    sales@flp.com.cn

ISBN 7-119-03070-1

©Foreign Languages Press, Beijing, China, 2002

Published by Foreign Languages Press
24 Baiwanzhuang Road, Beijing 100037, China

Distributed by China International Book Trading Corporation
35 Chegongzhuang Xilu, Beijing 100044, China
P.O. Box 399, Beijing, China

Printed in the People's Republic of China

Portrait of Zhuang Zi

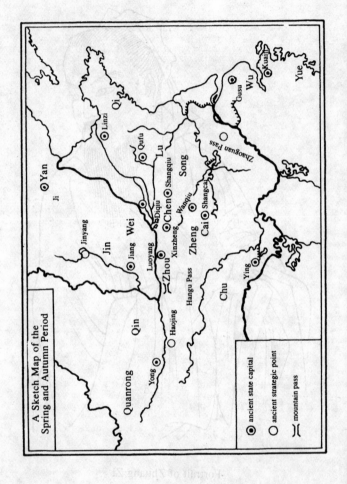

A Sketch Map of the Spring and Autumn Period

● ancient state capital
○ ancient strategic point
)(mountain pass

Contents

Foreword

The Spring and Autumn and Warring States
periods (770 BC-221 BC) were an epoch of great
upheavals in Chinese history. After more than 250
years, the vast area ruled by the Zhou Dynasty (c.
11th century BC-256 BC) was no longer peaceful
and prosperous, but was beset with crises. In 771
BC, the incompetent Zhou ruler, King You, was
killed during an invasion by the Quanrong tribe
from northwest China. Gaojing, his capital city
(located to the southwest of present-day Xi'an
City in Shaanxi Province) went into a decline, and
the dynasty lost half of its land and people.

In 770 BC, his successor, King Ping, was forced
to move the capital from the central Shaanxi plain
to Luoyi (Luoyang, in today's Henan Province) in
the east. This was the watershed which led histo-
rians to divide the dynasty into Western Zhou (c.
11th century BC-771 BC) and Eastern Zhou (770
BC-221 BC). Eastern Zhou itself is roughly divided into two historical periods. The former is

1

called the Spring and Autumn Period (770 BC-476 BC), and the latter is called the Warring States Period (475 BC-221 BC).

After the moving of the capital, the strength and prestige of the Zhou Dynasty declined disastrously, and the Zhou rulers lost all real control over the powerful dukes and princes, who ruled their territories as virtually independent fiefdoms.

The political and military struggles among the states ruled by the dukes and princes during the Spring and Autumn Period resulted in the dominance of the whole land by a handful of powerful states. The Warring States Period was thus ushered in, when these states — Qi, Chu, Yan, Han, Wei, Zhao and Qin — fought continual wars against each other and engaged in endless intrigue for hegemony.

In 221 BC, the State of Qin, having conquered all its rivals, abolished the Zhou Dynasty, which by that time existed in name only. The First Emperor of the Qin Dynasty, Qin Shi Huang, is regarded as China's first unifier, as he was the first man to rule just about all of what is present-day China.

Important changes took place in all aspects of Chinese society during the Spring and Autumn and Warring States periods. As the political situation changed from a rigid and ordered hierarchy under the "Son of Heaven" (the Zhou Emperor) to one in which powerful ministers and regional strongmen came to the fore, the function of the patriarchal system based on blood relations began to weaken. People began to lose their awe of Heaven and the gods, and the traditional religion and superstitions were increasingly questioned. As a result of the development of the social productive forces, the long-time social turbulence, the collapse of the patriarchal order and the rise of the status of the common people, the aristocratic monopoly on learning and culture was gradually broken. More and more private individuals began to give lectures, expounding their theories of the universe and education, and the way the empire should be governed. A welter of schools of thought arose, such as Confucianism, Mohism, Taoism, Legalism, Military Strategy, Logicism, Yin-Yang, Political Strategy, Agriculturism, and Electicism, to name but a few. This phenomenon, unmatched in Chinese history either before or since, has been described as one of "A hundred flowers blossom and a hundred schools of thought contend."

The works of theory and practical statecraft which have been handed down from these schools exerted a far-reaching and positive influence on the development of the philosophy and culture of later generations. At the same time, the different schools influenced each other, learned from each other and absorbed ideas from each other. They collectively made valuable achievements in the natural sciences, economics, literature and the arts, bequeathing an important legacy to the civilization of mankind.

Zhuang Zi (c. 369 BC-286 BC) was born with the given name Zhou in the State of Song. He is regarded as the chief representative of the Taoist school after Lao Zi. He attacked the official ideology of ritual, despised princes and dukes, refused to take an official post, and wandered all over the empire teaching his ideas. The book attributed to him, titled *The Book of Zhuang Zi*, has had a far-reaching influence through the ages with its forceful, natural and easy style, and wit and humor.

The Story of Zhuang Zi vividly portrays the great thinker's colorful life, interwoven with the historical incidents of his lifetime. It brings to life the splendor, tragedy and wonder of a distant age, with the intrigues and struggles of the mighty nobles, alongside the daily problems and thoughts of the common people.

Written as a popular literary biography, *The Story of Zhuang Zi* presents the principal features of Zhuang Zi's career, times and thought in the form of a novel. All the protagonists, incidents and cultural features presented here are taken from the original sources. It is, so to speak, a work of both literature and history.

Entering an Idyllic World

In the year 369 BC, the seventh year of the reign of Xi, King Lie of the Zhou Dynasty. Mt. Mengshan in the State of Song (spreading over the eastern part of present-day Henan Province, and parts of Shandong, Jiangsu and Anhui provinces) was covered with new greenery. Patterns of ripples rolled across the surface of Mengze Lake at the foot of the mountain, and the Menghe River ran like a white silk ribbon from half way down the mountain into the lake, completing a picture of refreshing beauty and repose.

No one would have guessed from this peaceful scene that the country was in turmoil, with the rulers of the major feudal states locked in deadly strife, sacking cities, ravaging the countryside and slaughtering the common people in a constant bloody struggle for supremacy.

Mengzhuang Village was a cluster of no more than a dozen houses situated on a small piece of flat land between the mountain and the lake. At the easternmost end of the village lived a family named Zhuang. The head of the household was called Zhuang Laogong (Gaffer Zhuang), the honorific title being bestowed upon him because in his younger days he had been the market supervisor in Suiyang, the capital city of the State of Song (south of present-day Shangqiu County in Henan Province). He had dealt with all kinds of petty peddlers, vendors, shops and stores from day to day. He had such a reputation for honesty and fairness that the market traders were happy to pay their taxes, and those whose business was slack were sure to be given time to pay. Whenever a dispute arose, both sides were happy to allow him to arbitrate.

Gaffer Zhuang was nearly 50 years old when he moved his family to Mt. Mengshan. His wife Hui Ming was a native of the area, and he was sure that, although he had become well accustomed to the bustle of the capital and its marketplace, the tranquility of the countryside would suit him well in his retirement.

Hui Ming had been the daughter of a shoe peddler. She lost her mother when she was still a child. She and her old father eked out a living by weaving shoes from fibers taken from reeds they gathered from the lake, and selling them in the market at Suiyang. This way, they became acquainted with Gaffer Zhuang.

One day, when Old Hui and his daughter were peddling their shoes in the market, one of the bodyguards of Duke Xiu, ruler of the State of Song, came strolling by. Impressed by the quality of the shoes, Wei — for this was his name — told his attendants to take them all. Old Hui's request for payment was met with jeers and threats, and when Hui Ming appealed to the bully, he was struck by her beauty, so he ordered his men to bring her along as well. At this juncture, as the other peddlers were grumbling in indignation, Gaffer Zhuang appeared.

At the sight of this top market official, the bodyguard started to fumble in his pockets for money to pay for the shoes, but found to his dismay that he had not brought his purse with him.

Gaffer Zhuang, wise to the ways of the world, took in the scene at a glance.

"I see that you are in the embarrassing situation of not having the money to pay for these exquisite shoes," he said, meaningfully. "But never mind. I will lend you the required sum, and you can pay me back later."

With that, he handed over to Hui Ming, who by this time had rushed back into her father's arms, enough money to pay for all the shoes they had brought with them that day.

As the bodyguard and his cronies slunk away

with their tails between their legs, Gaffer Zhuang paid Old Hui for his future products in advance and advised him to stay away from the market in future, as he would send men to pick up his shoes from home. The friendship between them thus started culminated in Gaffer Zhuang marrying Hui Ming.

When he retired at the age of fifty, Gaffer Zhuang already had a three-year-old son. Now his wife was expecting another baby soon. Early one spring morning, he took his fishing rod and walked to Mengze Lake, hoping to catch some fish to build up his wife's health. On the way, he reflected on how good life had turned out to be for him. He found that life away from the noisy and crowded city suited him well. He found endless pleasure in the mountains, woods, lake and river. He had a virtuous and clever wife at home, and was about to be blessed with another son in his late years. Gazing into the water of Mengze Lake, the first thing he saw was his beaming face.

Flocks of birds were sporting on the surface of the lake, shoals of fish were swimming near the surface, and ripples were chasing each other in giddy pursuit. Fish rose to the bait one after another, and eventually he landed a fine fat carp. Its scales glittered in the sunlight.

Gaffer Zhuang carefully took the hook from

its mouth. He had caught innumerable fish with that very same rod, but he had never seen one like this before. Its ruddy body was as slippery, fine and smooth as the skin of a newborn baby. He held the fish as if it were the embodiment of something good. He looked hard into the carp's eyes, and the carp looked tearfully back at the aging fisherman, as if they were communicating their innermost feelings.

After some time, Gaffer Zhuang bent, and mechanically, as if it were the most natural thing to do in the world, put the carp slowly back into the water. The fish swam once in a circle, seemingly as a gesture of thanks, and swam off in the crystal clear water of the lake.

No sooner had the fish disappeared than Gaffer Zhuang heard someone calling him. "Gaffer Zhuang, you should go straight home! You've got another bouncing baby boy!" It was one of his neighbors.

Coming out of his reverie, Gaffer Zhuang snatched up his fishing rod and the basket half-filled with the fish he had caught that morning, and hurried home. The sun had already climbed over the top of Mt. Mengshan. The whole mountain was enveloped with the singing of birds and the fragrance of flowers. Even the quiet track under his feet was dotted with innumerable flowers in all the colors of the rainbow. Naturally, an exquisite flower was also in full bloom in Gaffer Zhuang's heart too.

Hearing her husband come in, Hui Ming opened her eyes and smiled with joy, as if she had fulfilled an extremely solemn mission. Gaffer Zhuang bent over her, and put his face against hers, whispering with deep emotion:

"Thank you, my dear wife."

He held the baby in his arms, looked carefully at him for a moment and found the baby had a broad forehead and small but bright eyes. Beaming with joy, he said to Hui Ming, "His eyes are like mine, but his forehead is like that of my dear wife. He has the features of both of us. We'll call him Zhuang Zhou."*

Lying on the bed with her eyes exuding tenderness and love, Hui Ming nodded gently, stretched her arms out, and took the baby. She kissed the child, and said softly:

"Zhuang Zhou, Zhuang Zhou, my dear boy."

Zhuang Zhou made not a sound, but a faint smile flickered on his face.

---

*Zhuang Zhou is popularly known as Zhuang Zi in China, the word "zi" being an ancient title of respect for a learned or virtuous man or a man in general.

Laborious Confucian Studies

After kissing Hui Ming, Gaffer Zhuang, taking his elder son Zhuang Yan by the hand, left the house and climbed the mountain again.

Wild flowers were in bloom all over the slopes, and they could gather as many and of whatever kind as they pleased. The two of them picked a bundle of colorful and fragrant orchids, azaleas, roses and roses of Sharon, and brought them back for Hui Ming and her new baby in high spirits. She pulled the elder son Zhuang Yan over and kissed his little face again and again, with a smile to express her thanks to her husband. Gaffer Zhuang, for his part, went into the kitchen to prepare a thanksgiving feast.

Gaffer Zhuang and his wife had high ambitions for their two sons; the elder one would go into business, to provide wealth for the family, while the younger one would become a scholar, acquire an official post, and bring them all honor and fame. But their smug contentment was not to last long.

It was when Zhuang Zhou was nine years old. One snowy day, while hunting hares on the mountain, Gaffer Zhuang caught a bad cold. All the efforts of the best physicians — even ones from the capital — were not sufficient to stave off the old man's severe coughing, which developed vomiting of blood, and within a couple of weeks the old man died.

The loss of his beloved father cast a shadow over Zhuang Zhou, which he never shook off and which changed the course of his life.

His father's grave was beside a spring on Mt. Mengshan. Zhuang Zhou often visited it. Facing the green mound, he would stand there murmuring for a long time as if in conversation with his endlessly sleeping parent. Or he would indulge himself in reveries and let memories of his father doting on him come flooding back into his mind.

The change first manifested itself in his attitude to the studies which his father had been so keen for him to pursue. Although he attended school in a single-storied thatched building on the southern slope of Mt. Mengshan every day, and was diligent in performing his tasks, Zhuang Zhou found the lectures increasingly irksome. Since the great sage and educator Confucius (551 BC — 479 BC) had opened the first private school in China, many others had followed suit.

Indeed, the zeal for education, which was necessary if one was to become an official, had induced all the states of the empire to provide schools with board and lodging for aspiring scholars. The State of Qi (in what is now the northern part of Shandong Province) was especially noteworthy in this regard, having more than 2,000 such students in the reign of Duke Xuan (319 BC – 301 BC).

The school at which Zhuang Zhou studied had been started as a private school by the father of the present teacher, Mr. Zhang Kun. But when Dai Tang, who had been a pupil of Zhang Kun's father, rose to become the prime minister of the State of Song, the school became the beneficiary of lavish government support, making it known far and wide.

Old Mr. Zhang taught generation after generation of students, and what he taught was the never-changing teachings of Confucius. However, in the age of never-ending warfare and upheavals, and the increasing misery and poverty of the common people, a host of new ideas were springing up to challenge the tenets of Confucius and his followers, no matter how much the Confucian orthodoxy was sanctioned by scholars, officials and rulers.

Some of the upstarts advocated a spartan militarism as the only way to achieve unity, stability and prosperity in the turbulent empire; some preached a harsh application of the laws, in a school of thought known as Legalism; some advocated Taoism, involving non-action and a retreat from the world and all its troubles. There were also the Yin-Yang school and the school of Za Jia, an eclectic mixing of various ideas put forward by several of the new wave of teachers.

Meanwhile, in the midst of all this intellectual ferment, the State of Song slumbered on as a backwater in which the teachings of Confucius were revered as the timeless truths.

Zhuang Zhou was an intelligent boy, and was good at remembering everything he had read. Within a few years he had memorized all that Old Mr. Zhang Kun had taught him. However, the more he listened to the teacher expounding the Confucian precepts, the more disinterested he became.

One spring morning, he dawdled on his way to school. The fresh air, the straight green pines, the tall and slender bamboos, the lovely roses, the clusters of orchids and wild flowers in a riot of colors enchanted him. His feet unconsciously directed him to the shore of Mengze Lake. What a beautiful and gratifying scene it was! he thought to himself. How free and happy the works of Nature were! Then he mused:

"What are the Confucian teachings for? Don't they merely clear the way for the princes, dukes and nobles to ride roughshod over the common people?"

So thinking, instead of heading on for the school, Zhuang Zhou set his face toward Mengze Lake.

Zhuang Zhou saw a shoal of fish in the lake swimming toward him. The fish pursued each other, played with each other, swam to the east one moment and to the west the next, leapt above the surface and dived down into the crystal-clear depths. Wild ducks were sporting on the water in the distance. They were constantly flocking together and dispersing, flying into the air and diving into the water. They were even freer and light-hearted than the swimming fish. Watching all this, he thought:

"Spring has returned to the land; everything is fresh; birds fly and fish swim free of all care. What a wonderful scene!"

As he murmured this, Zhuang Zhou bent down to pick a wild flower of a golden color by the waterside, and sniffed at it. It was fragrant and fresh. He stretched out his hand to let the fish smell it too, but the fish swam away, shaking their tails, as soon as they saw his shadow and the yellow flower, leaving the water surface tranquil again.

With a sigh, he recollected that he was on his way to school. Bending his steps toward the schoolhouse, it was not long before he heard the drone of the other pupils reciting their lessons:

The Master said: "To subdue one's self and return to propriety, is perfect virtue. If a man can for one day subdue himself and return to propriety, all under Heaven will ascribe perfect virtue to him. Is the practice of perfect virtue from a man himself, or is it from others?"

"Great indeed was Yao as a sovereign! How majestic was he! It is only Heaven that is grand, and only Yao corresponded to it. How vast was his virtue! The people could find no name for it! How majestic was he in the works which he accomplished! How glorious in the elegant regulations which he instituted!"

"My doctrines make no way. I will get upon a raft, and float about on the sea. He that will accompany me will be Yu, I dare to say."

Listening to this litany, Zhuang Zhou muttered to himself:

"Where is there a man who has subdue his desires and returned to the rites? Which high official and noble lord has ever subdue his desires and returned to the rites? These stuffy old sentences simply urge the common people to resign themselves to their hard lives, and be content in the midst of exploitation! Confucius, you were truly an arch swindler deceiving the people! This Yao you praise so highly, like the others you hold up as paragons of virtue, was a figment of your own imagination. How pathetic!"

This thought stirred resentment in Zhuang Zhou's heart. He kicked open the door of the classroom, and entered. His school fellows fell silent, and stared at him wide-eyed. Mr. Zhang looked up. A frown creased his brows.

"Zhuang Zhou, you're late again!" he cried. "I know where you've been. Gazing at the scenery of Mengze Lake, am I right?"

Then his tone softened somewhat. "Zhuang Zhou," he said in a wheedling voice, "how do you expect to learn all you will need to know as a high official, an assistant to our sovereign, by staring blankly at trees, rocks and fish? Books are what you need to concentrate on. Books are treasure-houses of gold and jade. There is more beauty in books than in the uncomprehending world of Nature out there."

Zhuang Zhou put on a solemn face, and said:

"Sir, let me speak frankly. I think it's better for a man never to grow up. In his childhood, he is innocent, lively and sincere, but when he has the Confucian teachings instilled into him he gradually begins to parrot the sage's words. He forgets how to think and speak for himself, and becomes more hypocritical and fraudulent day after day. When he becomes an official or attains noble rank, he will advocate humanity, justice and virtue tirelessly to others, but behave just like a thief or other kind of scoundrel himself."

Both Mr. Zhang and the other students were stunned. But there was not one of them who was not aware of a new gleam of light stirring in his soul.

Commotion on Mt. Mengshan

A lengthy silence followed Zhuang Zhou's outburst. The teacher was lost in thought.

"Perhaps I have been blind," he wondered. "Perhaps I should permit my students to air their own views and talk of their own aspirations."

He had long known that Zhuang Zhou was one of the most intelligent boys in the class, and had suspected that the youth harbored unorthodox views. He coughed, and said:

"Well, boys, Zhuang Zhou has been impertinent, it is true. However, there should be room in every school for new and fresh opinions. So I want you now to tell me what your thoughts are on how you can attain your future goals."

The pupils had expected their teacher to give Zhuang Zhou a good scolding, and so his mild words caught them completely off guard. After a long pause, Hui Shi raised his hand. Given permission to speak by a nod from Mr. Zhang, the boy said:

"I think Zhuang Zhou is wrong. How can a

man never grow up? If all the people in the world do not grow up and stay boys and girls, who will govern the country, who will educate the others, who will cultivate the farms, and who will weave the cloth? Won't everyone starve to death?"

"Well, Zhuang Zhou?" said the teacher, with a smug grin. "What do you have to say to that?"

Zhuang Zhou did not hesitate. He replied:

"When I say it's better for a man never to grow up, I mean that a man is like the spring water on Mt. Mengshan, clear, pure, sweet and spotlessly clean in his childhood. As he gradually grows, he is like the water in the Menghe River, contaminated by withered twigs and fallen leaves, dead birds and rotting rodents. The taste of the water begins to change. When he is grown up, and especially when he learns the Confucian teachings, talks of humanity, justice and virtue, and enters society consisting of all kinds of people, he is like the water in Mengze Lake. It looks like a vast mirror, but under the surface are fish, turtles, shrimps, crabs, water snakes, leeches, mud and water weeds.

"A person lives a free life in childhood, his feelings are sincere and his morality is lofty, and he thinks and acts in the way his natural childhood instincts direct him. As he grows up, he learns to repeat what his seniors and teachers teach him. He is under pressure to act in the ways expected of him by his classmates and peers. He constantly quotes Confucius, and the ancient sage-kings Yao and Shun. He gradually departs from purity and innocence, and his moral sense and sentiments are at a lower level than before. Once he becomes an official, he betrays his conscience and childhood innocence, oppresses and robs the common people and puts himself in the service of ambitious and cruel lords whose only desire is to gain hegemony over his rivals, no matter how many people suffer in the process or how much the country is laid waste and impoverished. Aren't the morality and feelings of adults and people in power inferior to those of children?"

Zhuang Zhou's impassioned words moved his classmates. No sooner had he finished speaking than a burst of stormy applause filled the classroom. Even the old teacher found himself wondering if the words of Confucius, which he had been teaching for decades, did not now ring hollow. Disturbed, he looked round for someone to refute Zhuang Zhou. Cao Shang put up his hand, and Mr. Zhang eagerly urged him to speak.

Cao Shang was the son of Cao Bao, who was both an official and a wealthy trader in Suiyang. Cao Bao had sent his son to study at the school at

Mt. Mengshan, because it was the alma mater of Dai Dang, the current prime minister of the State of Song, and he hoped to advance his son's career thereby. Cao Shang had already spent five years at the school. He was 20 years old, and had already undergone the capping ceremony which marked the entrance to adulthood. He was tall, and had a refined and courteous manner, coupled with a lucid and clear style of speaking. He was a favorite of the old teacher. In debates, he always lost to Zhuang Zhou, but this time he was sure that he could triumph over his rival.

Cao Shang began:

"A real man should have extraordinary ability and a great ambition. This is my wish, a student's wish. Zhuang Zhou loves to live by the mountain and lake, and among the birds, flowers and insects. Isn't his the aspiration of a sparrow or the ambition of a farmer? Who looks after the fields, forests, lacquer plantations, and even carriages, boats, shops, stores, fish, salt, silk and cloth?

"It is the farmers, lacquer plantation workers, carriage drivers, fishermen, shop owners and weavers who look after them. But who will supervise these people of the lower classes? The junior officials, of course. But the junior officials are at the mercy of the higher officials. If you are born an outstanding man, if you are not a prince or a duke, you must be a prime minister. You are under one man, but above tens of thousands. When you venture out, you sit in a grand carriage pulled by fine horses. When you are indoors, you sit in a magnificent hall, discussing state affairs and enjoying whatever you please. Oh, how majestic is the manner in which you advance in your career! History will record your life in glowing terms!"

This pompous speech got a mixed reception. In the midst of the muttering and yawns, Hui Ze, an unassuming student, rose shyly, and spoke in a low, muffled voice. He said:

"Cao Shang has a great ambition to govern the state and to be a high-ranking official like our senior schoolmate Prime Minister Dai. It is an honor for our school and for our teacher Mr. Zhang. However, if everyone had such a lofty ambition, there would be no one to till the fields or look after the forests. The people would have neither clothes, nor food nor houses, and they would be worse off than the beasts, fish and insects. My father is a farmer. He urges me to learn from our teacher in the hope that I will have a career in government service and not be a farmer like him, because the life of the farmers is too hard...."

A sudden hubbub from afar interrupted Hui Ze's speech at this point. All heads turned in the direction of the door. The noise seemed to be coming from Mengzhuang Village. Zhuang Zhou, Hui Shi and Hui Ze rose, and, without asking the teacher's permission, trotted out of the classroom. They were soon followed by the other pupils, and eventually old Mr. Zhang himself strode out to see what the matter was.

It turned out that He Biao, the brother of Hui Ze's mother, had been arrested. He was a worker at the lacquer plantation on Mt. Mengshan. He had been an ordinary farmer drafted into military service. When he returned to his village after a dozen years or so, he learned that his wife and daughter had been both hounded to death by a lecherous local official and his land confiscated. All that was left to him was a small green grave. In order to earn a living, he became a worker at the lacquer plantation. But resentment continued to burn in his breast, and he had finally decided to take his revenge on the official who had so grievously wronged him. The latter, however, was forewarned, and fled. He Biao vented his rage by burning down the official's house, but was seized by soldiers sent from the capital just as he was about to leave the village.

Hui Ze reached home just in time to see his uncle bleeding from several wounds, his clothes tattered, being hustled along the street, tightly bound.

"Where are you taking my uncle?" cried Hui Ze, in dismay.

But before the soldiers could answer, He Biao spat, and barked:

"Hui Ze, don't reason with these hired thugs. This is a dark world, and despots are in power. There is no justice anywhere. Take good care of your mother. I am finished."

To Hui Ze, his uncle was a hero, a chivalrous man. After his father died, it was his uncle who had helped his family out. Today, despite this crushing adversity, his uncle was still a man of indomitable spirit.

At this moment, Zhuang Zhou hurried up. Seizing hold of a soldier, demanded:

"Have you arrested that brute of the despot who hounded He Biao's wife to death and killed his daughter? The murderer should pay with his life. Why don't you execute that brute of an official instead of arresting one of his victims?"

Appealing to the bystanders, he continued: "He Biao rendered outstanding service to the state. His body is covered with scars from the many battles he fought for our ruler and people. Now he is being arrested for an act of revenge after having been grievously wronged by a villainous official. I ask you, who are the real criminals? The officials, that's who! They wear the masks of benevolence, justice and morality, flaunt the banner of the sage Confucius and hold stately official posts. That so-called sage simply serves as a cloak to hide their appalling deeds of riding roughshod over the common people and bleeding them white!"

A storm of applause arose from the bystanders, both students and ordinary people alike. The soldiers hesitated, fearing the wrath of the crowd. Just at that moment, Mr. Zhang the teacher appeared. Calmly, he introduced himself to the captain of the guards, who immediately threw himself on the ground and kowtowed.

"Sir," he gasped, "it is such an honor to meet the teacher of our illustrious prime minister! Please forgive this disturbance, but I am only carrying out my orders in arresting this criminal."

Old Mr. Zhang said slowly, as if delivering a lecture: "The case involving He Biao has long been clear. He has suffered at the hands of a wayward official. Now, only when a penalty has been paid for a previous offence, can it serve as a warning for a subsequent one. The offending official should be brought to book first."

He went on:

"I will write a letter to the prime minister explaining the details of this case. That should absolve you of any blame, Captain. In the meantime, I suggest that you release your captive, and instruct your men not to molest my students."

The soldiers were only too pleased to escape from their predicament, and He Biao was set free.

After this, Mr. Zhang enjoyed prestige as never before in the eyes both of his students and of the people of Mengzhuang Village.

Butterfly in a Dream

Zhuang Zhou was even more dejected after the Mt. Mengshan incident. He became even more disgusted with Confucianism and the moral decadence of the time.

He no longer played truant, nor was he late for school again. He showed more respect for his teacher but the Confucian preaching and the oppressive atmosphere in the classroom wearied him.

One sultry summer morning, hardly had Mr. Zhang dismissed the class, when Zhuang Zhou bounded out of the door, with the feeling of escaping from a crowded sheepfold. He felt suddenly carefree in the scorching sun. He looked up, only to see birds, known and unknown, flying freely in flocks, in pairs or singly in the cloudless blue sky. Some flew out of the woods to the fields, to Mengze Lake and still farther; and some flew from the village, from the horizon and from the crops, singing and sporting, to the forests on Mt. Mengshan.

How happy and free they were! He thought of

himself and his classmates who were bound by ropes, both visible and invisible. The visible were not as terrible as the invisible ones, he thought. The dead hand of the Confucian teachings held their hearts in a chilling grip!

"Zhuang Zhou, you are in a trance again." Hui Ze, walking behind him, said, as he noticed him staring blankly at the sky.

"Hui Ze, you are my best friend," Zhuang Zhou replied. "I will tell you frankly I think that we are much worse off than the birds."

"But everyone knows that man is the wisest of all creatures!" protested his friend. "In what respect is a bird better off than a man? It spends all its life simply looking for food and avoiding enemies. It has natural enemies everywhere. Rainstorms hurt it, and ice and snow make it difficult for it to find food. It can be said to be in danger of death at every moment. Just by seeing a bird flying around freely in the blue sky on a fine day, we must not be misled into thinking that all its life consists of nothing but freedom."

"Hui Ze, where has your uncle gone?" Zhuang Zhou changed the subject.

"I don't know. I think he must be wandering far from home, or would have taken his revenge on that blackguard of an official," Hui Ze said dejectedly.

"When the lackeys are in power, the common people suffer!" commented Zhuang Zhou.

"I am most grateful to our teacher and you for your help in saving my uncle's life," said the other, unexpectedly.

"Let's not talk about it, Hui Ze. Would you like to go swimming in the lake?"

"All right," Hui Ze agreed with enthusiasm. "Let's forget all our worries, and go swimming. But I want you to promise to climb a tree and get some magpie's eggs for us to eat."

None of his classmates could match Zhuang Zhou in tree climbing, and he had long since proved how fearless he was. There was an old scholartree some scores of feet high in the courtyard of the school. Mr. Zhang one day got the idea that a flag flying from atop the tree would be a good way to advertise his school. But when he asked for volunteers to scale the tree and fix a flagpole and flag to its dizzy height, his pupils looked at each other anxiously, but said not a word.

But just then Zhuang Zhou arrived. When the teacher repeated his request, the lad straightaway offered to attempt the feat. He clambered up the old, gnarled tree as casually as if he had been walking along a well-paved road. Seemingly oblivious to the treacherous swaying of the topmost branches, he fixed the flagpole and flag in place, and shinned back down the tree in no time at all.

As Zhuang Zhou and Hui Ze were hurrying off to the lake, they were caught up by their classmate Hui Shi. He looked annoyed, not like he was ready to join them in their fun at all.

"I'm so disgusted!" he said, as soon as he caught up with the other two.

"Why, what's the matter?" chorused Zhuang Zhou and Hui Ze.

"I've just overheard Cao Shang asking Mr. Zhang what kind of a person Prime Minister Dai is, and what his likes and dislikes are," explained Hui Shi. "I'll bet he's going to write a fawning letter to the prime minister and beg for his favor. Disgraceful! If you want to take an official post and be successful, you must depend on your ability, not on flattery."

"My dear fellow, let's not worry about base toads like Cao Shang on a beautiful day like this," Zhuang Zhou urged, with a laugh. "Come swimming with us, and throw all your worries and gloom into Mengze Lake to feed the turtles!"

The sun was scorching. There had been no rain for a long time, and the road was covered with a thick layer of dust. It was as soft as wheat flour to the feet. The ears of the crops on both sides of the road were mostly curled and drooping, and a lot of the farmland was uncultivated and deserted, except for a few stooped and emaciated peasants scratching at the soil.

The splashes made by the three friends as they jumped into Mengze Lake startled a flock of water birds, which flew away screeching into the distance.

Zhuang Zhou swam to his heart's content, luxuriating in the delicious coolness of the water. Eventually he climbed out onto the bank, and joined the other two lying on the meadow grass, which felt as soft as a cotton blanket. He covered his body with his clothes, and enjoyed the embrace of Nature, experiencing a rare and exhilarating sense of peace of mind.

A gray bird suddenly hopped to his side. It was not a particularly beautiful creature, but it showed a surprising fearlessness. Before long, it had perched on the palm of his hand, chirping now and then, and pecking at his fingers. Zhuang Zhou found its attentions pleasant.

Unexpectedly, the bird scrambled along his arm, and looked him right in the face. Zhuang Zhou looked at the bird, while the bird looked at him. Two eyes met two eyes. In the bird's eyes Zhuang Zhou's face was reflected, and in Zhuang Zhou's eyes the whole bird was reflected.

Zhuang Zhou had never felt so happy before.

Not making the slightest movement, he allowed the bird to hop onto his face and even peck lightly at his blinking eyes in an exploratory way. He lay quietly for fear that it would fly away and that this beautiful time would vanish for ever. However, a breeze sprang up, rustling the leaves of the nearby trees. The bird spread its wings, and flew away from him.

Zhuang Zhou was unable to extricate himself from this beautiful state of mind. He continued to lie on the soft grass, absolutely still, eyes closed, shutting the vulgar world out completely from his mind, leaving only a spring from Mt. Mengshan in his heart, clear, transparent, pure and unpolluted by a single speck.

Gradually, he forgot the passing of the time, the eyes of the bird, Confucius' teachings, his mother and elder brother, and Hui Shi, Hui Ze — and Zhuang Zhou himself too....

He seemed to shake off all physical encumbrances and encirclements, and finally became a butterfly. The butterfly was not particularly striking, but it had two gossamer wings, a long neck and a graceful body. In raptures, it spread its wings and began to fly. It flew and flew, sometimes with its companions, sometimes alone. How happy and free it was! At one moment, it hovered over a field made golden with rape flowers in full

bloom; at another, it flew to the flowering shrubs in the vastness of the wilderness. Now soaring in a mountain valley blanketed with woods; now fluttering its wings in the vast blue sky. Aloft, it gazed down over the endless sea, then it shot to earth and probed into the very essence of a flower. It chatted with the bees and raced with the birds. It flew on to the peonies, crouched and slept on a rose leaf, played on the head of a monkey and dried itself on the back of a buffalo. With a pair of wings, it could go anywhere it pleased and do anything it liked.

How free and easy! What a delight!

But flying to and fro around a tall kapok tree, spreading its beautiful wings to vie with the red kapok flowers for beauty, suddenly there came a bleak gust of wind. The sky seemed blotted out, and the land became blurred; the kapok flowers fell one after another onto the ground, and the tree's branches snapped. The butterfly was blown into the sky — way above the clouds — and then fell heavily, its wings shattered, on to a thorny undergrowth, its whole body covered with cuts and bruises, and bleeding....

Zhuang Zhou opened his eyes abruptly. Hui Shi and Hui Ze were spraying the white juice from lotus roots in his face. He was still lying on the grass, and not in some thorny undergrowth, but the sun was nearing noon and his feet were no longer in the shade. He felt his body for injuries, but there were none.

He jumped to his feet, and wiped his face, evoking a burst of laughter from Hui Shi and Hui Ze.

"Zhuang Zhou, eat some of this crisp, cool lotus root!" Both Hui Shi and Hui Ze gave him a piece of lotus root.

"You two have disturbed my butterfly dream. Give me back my butterfly dream quickly!"

Hui Shi and Hui Ze were baffled. They stopped smiling, and asked simultaneously:

"What on earth is a butterfly dream?"

Zhuang Zhou explained:

"Just now, I dreamed that I was a butterfly, flying gay and carefree, flitting from flower to flower. Then suddenly you cast the butterfly down from the lofty skies to the hard and cruel ground. Now you made me become Zhuang Zhou again. You are really a wet blanket!"

Friendship Spanning Generations

After his remarkable dream, Zhuang Zhou found the Confucian teachings duller and drier than ever. He was avid for the beautiful realm of Nature and more interested in the romantic charm of natural scenery than in dusty school books.

One day, he was sitting by Mengze Lake on the very spot where he had had the butterfly dream. He was strumming a lute, and singing to himself:

> O Phoenix! O Phoenix! How your virtue has declined!
> The life to come waits for no man, what is gone is gone.
> If goodness prevails in the world, the sage succeeds,
> If evil prevails, the sage lives freely.

The playing and singing were in complete harmony, like the flowing of a tiny stream at one moment and like the soughing of the wind in the pines at another; it was like the coming of a sudden storm alternating with bright sunshine.

Zhuang Zhou was completely absorbed in his music, giving tongue to his anxiety at the state of the world, and at the same time revealing his longing for a beautiful life.

"Young man!" A voice like the morning bell brought him back to earth. Zhuang Zhou opened his eyes and saw an old fisherman sitting facing him. He scrambled to his feet, and greeted the stranger politely.

"Your playing is melodious and refreshing, and your singing is free and easy. Where are you studying?" The old fisherman asked, in a low but firm voice.

"Thank you for your comment. I'm studying under the tutorship of Mr. Zhang of Mt. Mengshan."

"What does your teacher teach?"

"Nothing but benevolence, justice and virtue, poems, history, rites and music, as preached by Confucius."

"Young man, benevolence, justice and virtue are the root of all the trouble in the world. In fact, things of the same kind are attracted to each other, birds of a feather flock together, and like attracts like. In the past, before the sage came into the world, there was no high or low, and the people lived a carefree and roving life, without

40

autumn or winter. Harmony prevailed everywhere, and people treated each other equally and fairly. At that time, there were no roads in the mountains, no boats or bridges on the waters, and the crowing of the cocks and the barking of the dogs were clearly heard from village to village. Nobody hurt anyone else; in fact, a child could pull the tail of a tiger without being injured. When a boy climbed a tree to look at a magpie's nest, the magpie would chirp to express its welcome to him. At that time, there was no difference between the ruler and the ruled, no difference between the exalted and the lowly. There was no bullying, nor was there oppression. Following their natural instincts, the people were simple and sincere, and had no desires. Therefore, they were noble-minded."

Hardly had the old fishermen finished speaking, when Zhuang Zhou jumped to his feet in excitement. He took the fisherman by the hand, and gasped.

"Hearing your words is better than studying in school for ten years! You've laid bare the essence of the sage's so-called benevolence, justice and virtue with one penetrating remark. You've said what I have long wanted to say but didn't say. You've portrayed a beautiful realm, which I've always sought, but didn't know where to look.

Whenever I tried to express myself in the past, some people said I was talking nonsense, some said I was ambitious, and some even said I was an idiot or a fool. Today, I find your state of mind is much higher than mine. You have a broader mind than I do. You are the real sage. You are the teacher of my heart!"

"Zhuang Zhou, when the sounds are the same, they become harmonious," the old fisherman replied. "My words were in harmony with the tune you played on your lute, that is all."

"Sir, I would like to have you point the way for me," Zhuang Zhou said, with a humble bow.

The other resumed:

"The reason why the Confucian views are absurd and wrong is that they ignore the facts, making arbitrary comments to deceive the common people. When farmland is uncultivated, the households are ruined, no distinction is maintained between seniors and juniors, and the taxes are not paid. This is what the ordinary people should worry about. When a person is unable to do what he wishes, his behavior is dishonorable, and he becomes indolent and neglectful of his duties. This is what the officials should worry about. When the country is in chaos, the royal court is in disorder, a skilled worker is no longer skilful, the tributes and taxes are not sufficient, and the Son of Heaven is not pleased. This is what the princes and dukes should worry about. When dukes and princes rebel, they fight each other, the people are plunged into an abyss of misery, the Yin and Yang are no longer in balance, there is no restraint on the rites and music, and the country runs short of financial resources. This is what the Son of Heaven should worry about.

"Confucius did not have the same power and influence as the sovereigns, princes and dukes above, nor did he have the same official ranks and posts as the ministers below, but he promoted the rites and music, dictated what human relations should be and told the common people how to behave, without having the authority to do so. Therefore, what he said was aimless and can only disgust the people!"

"Exactly!" cried Zhuang Zhou, clapping his hands.

"Zhuang Zhou, the reason why Confucius could not civilize the common people is that he himself could not get rid of the eight evil habits and four harms afflicting the people. How could he hope to civilize the common people and be called a sage?"

"Would you teach me please?" Zhuang Zhou begged.

"What are the eight evil habits? If you do

what is not your business to do, it is called usurpation. If you give advice before you understand the other party's position, it is called importunity. If you speak at the will of another, it is called flattery. If you put in a good word for another person to show respect for his feelings without telling right from wrong, it is called submission. If you are keen on commenting on other's faults, it is called slander. If you sow dissension among good friends, it is called causing harm to others. If you praise the swindler and defame the honest man, it is called craftiness. If you do not distinguish good from evil, act in a double-dealing way and fawn on both sides for your own ends, it is called insidiousness.

"These eight evil habits are more than enough to mislead the people outside you and hurt the heart inside you. A gentleman will not make friends with a person who displays any of these traits, nor will a wise sovereign appoint him as a minister.

"What are the four harms? If you are fond of doing important tasks and spurn ordinary tasks in order to achieve success and fame, this is called grasping. If you monopolize knowledge, make arbitrary decisions on matters, infringe on others' rights and interests, and like to show off your own abilities, this is called avarice. If you do not curb your bad habits and mend your ways when you see your own faults, and your faults become more serious when you listen to other's advice, this is called perverseness. If you are pleased with those who agree with you and regard those who do not agree with you as bad people, even if they are good people, this is called conceitedness.

"Didn't Confucius display these eight evil habits and four harms? Not only did he have them, but they were conspicuous. How could he civilize the common people? Therefore, when he traveled to the various states, no one was attracted by what he preached. This was why he was driven out of the State of Lu twice, fled from the State of Wei, was attacked in the State of Song and found himself in dire straits in the states of Chen and Cai."

This profound, clear-cut and penetrating analysis and criticism coming from a simple fisherman whisked Zhuang Zhou into an entirely new realm. It was a realm no one had ever set foot in before. But with the fisherman as his guide, the two of them had entered it. Zhuang Zhou was intoxicated with excitement, and forgot everything around him.

After pondering over what the fishermen had said, Zhuang Zhou asked him:

"Sir, why didn't Confucius stop before going

too far, instead of persisting in obstinacy?"

Stroking his white beard, the fishermen said:

"That's a good question. The reason why he obstinately stuck to his own course was that he had sunk in it too deep to extricate himself. It is just like a man who is afraid of his own shadow or dislikes his own footprints. When he wants to cast them off, he keeps running desperately. However, the farther he runs, the faster the shadow runs after him, and the more he moves his feet, the more footprints he makes. As a result, he continuously accelerates until he dies of exhaustion. Confucius should have known that if he stood under a big tree or in a dark place and calmed himself, there would have been neither shadow nor footprints!"

"How wonderfully penetrating and apt!" Zhuang Zhou cried, dancing for joy like a child.

Zhuang Zhou went on to ask, after pondering for a while:

"Then what kind of big tree can make the people all over the world naturally lofty without seeking benevolence, justice, rites and wisdom?"

The fishermen replied:

"The solution is to preserve the original truth and seek the world of supreme virtue. The original truth means the extremity of refined purity and honesty. The world of supreme virtue refers to the time when there was no distinction between the eminent and the humble or between the above and the below in the absence of the sage.

"Young man, I haven't said this for more than 30 years. Today, when I heard your playing and singing, I felt that I had met a young friend, a rare friend who is well versed in music. That is why I've poured out these words which are at odds with the current customs, as an exchange of views between us!"

"Sir, you are a true sage!" was Zhuang Zhou's ardent comment. "You are precisely the teacher I've been longing for day and night. Please accept my obeisance."

"Zhuang Zhou, let's become close friends despite the big difference in our ages," said the fisherman, turning and walking to the shore of the lake. There, he stepped onto a small boat, and before Zhuang Zhou could catch up with him, pushed the boat off from the bank with a long bamboo pole. In no time at all, the fisherman and his boat had vanished into the vastness of Mengze Lake

From then on, Zhuang Zhou found that his eyes had been opened to the sordidness of the ways of the world, and had an even keener awareness of the hypocrisy of Confucius and his teachings.

From then on, Zhuang Zhou often went back to Mengze Lake, and paced up and down where he and the old fisherman had met. He was eagerly hoping that the other would appear again, so that he could learn more genuine knowledge and pour out to him the melancholy in his heart.

One afternoon, after school, the sun was setting in the west, and the lotus flowers had turned into lotus seedpods, protruding from or hanging down above the surface of the lake. Just when Zhuang Zhou was giving up hope that the old fisherman would come, and was about to go home, when the old man's boat glided up to the shore of the lake.

The two of them greeted each other like old friends as soon as the old man had sprung lightly ashore, and gazed into each other's eyes as they stood hand in hand.

"I've caught some nice fish today," The old man broke the silence. "I would like to invite you to partake of fish soup at my house."

Zhuang Zhou was overjoyed at the invitation. The old fisherman helped him aboard the boat, and then poled away across the lake.

As he sat in the gently rocking boat, Zhuang Zhou was filled with delight as he gazed at the woods on Mt. Mengshan, the sequestered villages, the screen-like reed marshes, the rosy clouds in the sky and the birds returning to their nests in the afterglow.

The old fisherman's two-room thatched hut was located on a hillock by the lake, surrounded by dense woods. A horse looked up from its grazing, and whinnied a welcome to the young stranger.

While he was lighting the fire and preparing the fish soup, the old fisherman chatted animatedly. Zhuang Zhou heard many new tales, in which was embedded a wealth of historical, geographical, natural and human knowledge. He found out that the people extolled as worthies in the stories from ancient times were in fact not benevolent or righteous at all. He also learned that none of the truly benevolent, righteous and loyal officials and subjects died natural deaths.

The two of them talked frankly and enthusiastically over bowls of delicious soup, forgetting the passing of the time and everything around them.

When they became aware of their surroundings again, they found a bright moon hanging in the sky, flooding everything on earth with a silvery white. With regret, the old fisherman said it was time that he should ferry Zhuang Zhou back to the other shore of the lake.

The two stood on the shore, reluctant to part. The old fisherman said:

"Zhuang Zhou, we have now become good friends despite the big difference in our ages."

"Yes, dear old uncle," Zhuang Zhou replied without hesitation.

The bright moon and the stars dotting the sky hung like lanterns, showing the old fisherman and Zhuang Zhou their respective ways back home.

The First Pilgrimage

Zhuang Zhou became more mature and thoughtful after his chat with the old fisherman. He found he had a deeper understanding of what Confucius meant by benevolence, justice and virtue. He also had a clearer idea of the role of the Son of Heaven, and of the princes and dukes who ruled the various states. But most of all, he began to understand the root causes of the hardships of the common people.

Round about this time, Dai Dang, the prime minister of the State of Song, came to his old school to personally select promising young men for government service.

It was almost a foregone conclusion that Cao Shang would be chosen, for he had brought himself to the prime minister's attention by means of flattering missives. Cao Shang's father, too, had pulled strings at court. Zhuang Zhou, however, when he was examined by the prime minister, had expounded on the old and heterodox text "Dao Zhi Scathingly Denounces Confucius." This incident, in fact served to make Zhuang Zhou's name known far and wide, not only in the State of Song, but also far beyond its borders.

Cao Shang was well aware that he could not match Zhuang Zhou so far as learning and literary talent were concerned; nor was he as good as Hui Shi in genuine knowledge and eloquence. But now that he had been chosen to join the elite ruling class, he was puffed up with conceit and self-confidence. Just before he left the school to embark on what he thought would be an illustrious career, he approached Zhuang Zhou, and said, smugly:

"I would like to give you a word of advice, Zhuang Zhou. Your natural gifts and literary talent are unparalleled, but they'll lie fallow all your life unless you mend your ways and treat your superiors with the deference due to them. Curb your hasty temperament, and measure your words with care, and perhaps in the future you may outgrow your immaturity, and achieve a modicum of success."

Zhuang Zhou replied:

"The two of us have different or even entirely opposite views on the doctrines of Confucius. We have studied together in the same room for five years. We are classmates and friends, surely. Everyone must follow his own path. That which leads to officialdom is not mine, so I'm afraid that your advice to me to restrict my natural inclination to be outspoken has fallen on stony ground.

"Now you are about to join the ranks of the people who rule the state. I sincerely hope that you will resist the temptation to accept bribes and oppress the common people like so many officials do. But I am afraid you may have got off to a bad start, for it is said that you owe your promotion to nothing other than you father's influence. Is that true?"

At this point, Hui Shi chimed in:

"I have heard that too."

Cao Shang reddened, but before he could deny the accusation, Zhuang Zhou said, in a conciliatory tone:

"No matter what people say, your understanding of 'benevolence' suits Prime Minister Dai's taste. Someone must be chosen for the job of administering the state."

The three were thoughtful for a while, and then Hui Shi said:

"The three of us, plus Hui Ze, each have different ambitions. As for Zhuang Zhou, he is interested in mountains and waters, and makes no attempt to do anything. As for Cao Shang, he hankers after rank and riches. As for Hui Ze, he is honest and simple, and will be content to farm his ancestral land. As for me, I am an empty-headed talker; who would hire me?"

This prompted Zhuang Zhou to say:

"What you say is correct in some respects, but not in all. You must realize that doing nothing means doing something, and that doing something means doing nothing."

This mysterious comment seemed to relieve Cao Shang, for he said, "The three of us are now at the junction of three roads. Let's each take our own road, and look forward to meeting again."

Zhuang Zhou said musingly:

"Today, the shameless are wealthy, the peddlers of deceit hold prominent posts, and the followers of Confucius are in the ascendant everywhere. It's clear that wealth, prominence and glory are not my lot."

After a thoughtful pause, he went on:

"Cao Shang, you mentioned that we are about to embark on three different roads. Originally, there were no roads in the world. It was only when people went their different ways that roads appeared. And more roads will be trampled out in future, as people seek different goals."

The three friends parted, and Zhuang Zhou walked in the direction of the lake, which seemed to have a magnetic attraction for him.

As he walked along, lost in thought, he stumbled over a tree root, and fell headlong. The commotion frightened a hedgehog, which curled itself up into a ball not far from Zhuang Zhou's face. The boy stared blankly at the hedgehog, and lay quietly on the wet fallen leaves until the hedgehog came to the conclusion that there was no longer any danger, poked its head out, uncurled its body, flattened its spines, and crawled slowly away. Zhuang Zhou had a flash of inspiration, and said, as if reciting a lesson:

"Every man has his own road; every animal has its own skill; and everything has its form. Why not let Nature take its course and let every creature compete for freedom? Why must there be princes, dukes and officials, and the hidebound Confucian doctrines? What makes the princes and dukes superior to the hedgehog? Where is the doctrine that the hedgehog must learn to obey?"

Wandering for the rest of the day in raptures through the thick woods on Mt. Mengshan, Zhuang Zhou held dialogues with the trees, bandied questions and answers with the birds, make inquiries of the flowers, and lectured the insects. Not until the sun doused itself in Mengze Lake did he return home.

Cao Shang's selection for a post at the court of

Duke Ticheng, ruler of Song, proved to be a watershed in the life of Hui Shi. The corruption and decadence of the dominant Song aristocracy stifled all hope of reform, Hui Shi concluded. He must seek an enlightened monarch to whom he might expound his ideas of good government. After much thought, he decided to try his luck in the State of Wei (covering parts of present-day Shanxi, Henan, Shaanxi and Hebei provinces).

Marquis Wen of Wei (r.445 BC — 396 BC) had made a wise move in appointing a man called Li Kui as prime minister. Li Kui's reforms had resulted in Wei becoming a power to match the mighty states of Qin, Chu and Qi. However, it had been locked in a military stalemate with the State of Qi to its east for a dozen years or so, as a strategist of genius, Sun Bin, grandson of Sun Wu, the author of the famous military treatise *Sun Zi's Art of War*, advised the Qi ruler.

Sun Bin's counterpart at the Wei court was his erstwhile classmate Pang Juan. Fully aware that Sun Bin was far superior to himself in matters of military science, and fearing an ominous challenge from the State of Qi, Sun Bin's homeland, if the latter were to be appointed adviser to the Qi ruler, Pang Juan inveigled his old comrade to visit him in Wei. Once there, Sun Bin found himself arrested, tortured and his kneecaps removed. But before Pang Juan could have him killed, Chunyu Kun, an envoy from Qi, smuggled Sun Bin back home. Appointed chief strategist to the ruler of Qi, Sun Bin put all his energies into the destruction of Wei.

When Zhuang Zhou was 18 years old (in 353 BC), Wei attacked the State of Zhao, which requested help from Qi. Sun Bin saw his opportunity immediately. Instead of sending reinforcements to Zhao itself, he attacked Wei directly. The poorly defended capital of Wei soon fell, and the Wei army in the field was cut off from assistance. Wei suffered a crushing defeat.

Hui Shi thought that the State of Wei, having experienced the futility of war, would be ripe for conversion to the ways of peace through internal harmony. He consulted Zhuang Zhou about his plan, but his friend was skeptical.

"You may find King Hui of Wei less susceptible than you think to your arguments," he said, shaking his head. "All the princes and dukes want to take as much land as possible from other states so as to increase their own spheres of influence, without losing any of their own. They care nothing about the sufferings of the people."

"But new wounds are painful," rejoined Hui Shi. "Now is the time to approach King Hui, and explain how the arts of peace and benevolent government will in the end make his state invulnerable, because it will be shored up by the might of the common people."

Zhuang Zhou mulled over this for a while, and then said:

"By the way, I too have decided to leave Song."

He then told Hui Shi of his meeting with the old fisherman:

"The old man told me that the State of Chu, and the southern part of that state in particular, is a place with beautiful mountains, beautiful waters and beautiful people. The influence of Confucius and his doctrines is but slight in that southern land. Its people are still honest and simple, and maintain the highest virtue, he said. So I've decided to go there and see for myself."

So saying, he gazed high into the sky toward the south.

Parting from Hui Shi, Zhuang Zhou walked around the lake to the old fisherman's thatched hut. A delicious odor of frying fish wafted from the doorway of the old man's abode.

"Somehow I knew you were coming, and so I am preparing a farewell feast for you," the old man chuckled when he saw Zhuang Zhou approaching.

As he fed the fire and turned the fish on the stove, he said:

"By the way, I've heard that Cao Shang has left to take an official post at court. Have you any idea what you wish to do next?"

"Yes. I've made up my mind to travel to the south."

The old fisherman nodded in approval. "That is a good idea. The states of Chu and Yue are still relatively untouched by the decay which has infected the states of the Central Plain."

They chatted animatedly — the one excited at the prospect of exploring the unknown world outside, and the other proud of his courageous protege. The old fisherman told Zhuang Zhou of the route to the State of Chu, and explained its geographical conditions and customs. Then he took a small cloth bag down from a hook, and poured out a pile of colorful shells of various shapes, including genuine shells and ones made of copper. They bore inscriptions in an unfamiliar language. He told him that it was the shell money used in the State of Chu, equivalent to the knife money and cloth money used in the Central Plain. With it, he could buy all kinds of daily necessities. The inscriptions on the shells indicated their different values. Saying that money had long ceased to be of any use to him, the old fisherman pressed Zhuang Zhou to take the shells. He also gave him his horse.

"I am far too old nowadays to be gadding about on horseback," he said ruefully. "This animal will be your faithful companion when you have no other on your long journey."

Zhuang Zhou's mother received the news of her son's intention to wander down to the land of the "southern barbarians" with trepidation and alarm, instead of setting out on madcap wanderings. Besides, she reminded him, it was high time he got married.

"Your brother already has a five-year-old son," she remarked. But she knew she was fighting a losing battle with her strong-willed son.

The following morning Zhuang Zhou and his mother said a tearful farewell, and the young man cantered off into the early morning mist.

Overnight in the Wilderness

The further southward he journeyed, the fewer the people and the more thinly scattered the villages.

One day, he came upon a vast expanse of wilderness just as the sun was setting. There was an eerie silence upon the land, not even the crow of a rooster, and Zhuang Zhou shuddered to find that the only inhabitants of this barren place were skeletons of people who had come to no good end. He became aware that he had entered the territory of the former states of Chen and Cai. These had been small states which had prospered before the never-ending internecine wars for hegemony had broken out between the powerful states. Chen and Cai were trampled into the dust, separately in 479 BC and 447 BC, beneath the hooves of the war steeds of King Hui of the State of Chu. This erstwhile peaceful and thriving plain had become a place of slaughter where Chu vanquished one foe after another.

Skeletons bleached the land as far as the eye

could see. Some were complete; some had no legs or no arms; some had no heads; some were the remains of grown men, but others, alas, were certainly those of innocent children!

Not all had been killed in battle, Zhuang Zhou mused. Bad as the wars were, he knew, cruel punishments for petty crimes were practiced in many of the states, under the influence of the Legalist school. The latter preached that man was inherently evil, and only stern sanctions could make him follow the path of righteousness. Beheading, torture and dismemberment were common penalties. As if that were not enough, Zhuang Zhou thought sadly, famine stalked in the wake of war; many of these people had probably starved or frozen to death. The skeletons lay in various postures. Not a few had their arms stretched out, as if they had died begging for food, or for mercy. Some lay in groups, some alone, some lying against each other as if huddling together for warmth.

A chilly wind from the northwest accompanied the sunset. It drove masses of clouds that covered the land with a black mourning veil. Zhuang Zhou stumbled along through the bones and boulders that impeded his path. He had to lead his frightened horse and urge it onward. Before long, a flash of lightning heralded a thunderstorm, which raged above the forlorn traveler. Lashed by rain and hailstones as he struggled to leave the sinister plain behind him, Zhuang Zhou sang to vent his feelings for the deplorable situation of the time, as well as to keep his spirits up.

Gradually, the storm subsided, and the angry clouds floated away, revealing a bright moon and a sky studded with stars. Zhuang Zhou found himself exhausted and hungry. "I must find shelter," he thought, "even if I have to spend the rest of the night on this accursed wilderness."

It was then that he saw a thatched shed on a hillside. Making for it, he found that the floor was covered with a layer of soft, dry grass. There was fine pasture near the shed, too. So he let his horse graze freely, while he himself entered the shed, lay down, and in no time at all was fast asleep.

He did not know how long he had slept before he was wakened by a voice saying, "Zhuang Zhou, why do you lie on my body?"

Zhuang Zhou sat up, startled. He felt in the grass upon which he was lying — sure enough, there were human bones embedded in the ground. Springing out of the hut, he saw a skull on the ground facing him. Zhuang Zhou addressed the skull thus:

"Sir, was it some insatiable ambition that drove you to transgress the law, and brought you to this?

Was it the fall of a kingdom, the blow of the executioner's axe that brought you to this? Or had you done some shameful deed and could not face the reproaches of father and mother, of wife and child, and so were brought to this? Was it hunger and cold that brought you to this, or was it that the springs and autumns of your span had in their due course carried you to this?"

The skull did not reply. Zhuang Zhou then took it, and went back to sleep in the shed, with the skull for a pillow.

In the dead of the night, Zhuang Zhou seemed to hear the skull speaking to him in a dream:

"All that you said to me — your glib, commonplace chatter — is just what I should expect from a live man, showing as it does in every phrase a mind hampered by trammels from which we dead are entirely free. Would you like to hear a word or two about the dead?"

"I certainly would," said Zhuang Zhou.

The skull said:

"Among the dead, none is king, none is subject. There is no division of the seasons; for us, the whole world is spring, the whole world is autumn. No monarch on his throne has joy greater than ours."

Zhuang Zhou did not believe this.

"Suppose," he said, "I could get the Clerk of

Destinies to make your frame anew, to clothe your bones once more with flesh and skin, send you back to father and mother, wife and child, friends and home. I do not think you would refuse."

A deep frown creased the brow of the skull.

"How can you imagine," it asked, "that I would cast away joy greater than that of a king upon his throne, only to go back to the toils of the world of the living?"

Then a host of skeletons appeared.

One said:

"That is right. We can now live as long as Heaven and Earth, with no worries. Why should we give it up? Zhuang Zhou, I was a general of the State of Chen. I braved every kind of danger in order to get recognized and promoted. Laden with anxieties as I was, every day was like a year. I was showered with glory and wealth, and obtained power and rank. However, the wars never ended. In the course of them Chen fell to the State of Chu, and I with it, shot in the back by an arrow from a treacherous subordinate. Now, I'm neither afraid of the Chu army's ferocious charge, nor of my sovereign's frown. Gentlemen and villains, generals and foot soldiers, they all lie here without any difference in rank between them. There is no more cheating or deception, no more deceiving superiors or browbeating subordinates. All is perfect fairness and harmony at last."

Another skeleton pushed itself forward, and said:

"I was formally the sovereign of the State of Chen. All my waking hours were spent scheming how to increase my territory, how to thwart the schemes of Chu, how to make my subjects docile and fearful, how to obtain the best of food and wine, beautiful women, jewelry, and magnificent pavilions for my enjoyment, and how to prolong my life. Now, however, I don't bother my head about such trifles any more. Heaven has granted me peace. The burden of kingship has been lifted from me forever."

A third butted in:

"I was a wealthy landowner. I thought I had everything a man could desire. But the constant worry that someone would steal from me my property, wives and treasures sapped my health. In my helpless state, others tricked me out of all that I had striven so hard to acquire, and I died penniless. Yet, who would have thought that in the land of the dead, where I have nothing, that I would find true contentment?"

While listening to this discourse, Zhuang Zhou found his face itching — and awoke to find a mosquito biting him. He looked at the skull he had used for a pillow, half expecting it to say something. But not a sound did it make.

As he left the shed and emerged into the gray light of dawn, his horse ran up and nuzzled him affectionately. Zhuang Zhou patted its flanks, glad to have a companion in this dreary place, where he had gained a profound insight into the nature of death.

The Friendly People of the State of Chu

Leaving the haunted desolation which had once been the states of Chen and Cai, and continuing southward, Zhuang Zhou found the land gradually becoming more lush and green. More and more streams and rivers appeared, until there were fewer land routes than waterways.

Perceiving that he would soon have to start travelling by boat, Zhuang Zhou decided, with a heavy heart, that he would have to leave behind his faithful horse. At a place called Yancheng, where there was a wide expanse of grassland, he stripped the horse of its bridle, reins and saddle. The horse seemed to understand that this was the final parting of their ways, and trotted off obediently when Zhuang Zhou whispered a fond word of farewell in its ear.

Not far off was a ferry. The boatman was an old man with finely chiseled features and a white beard that flowed down over his chest. He smiled as he waved Zhuang Zhou aboard, and immediately cast off from the shore, poling the boat with sturdy strokes. Just as they reached the middle of the river Zhuang Zhou was startled out of a melancholy reverie by the neighing of a horse. Looking up, astonished, he saw his faithful steed perched on the top of a steep cliff. He frantically waved to signal the animal to retreat from the edge of the precipice, but instead of obeying him, the horse plunge down into the river, just ahead of the ferry boat.

Scarcely knowing what he was doing, Zhuang Zhou jumped into the water too, and swam to the horse. Then the two of them made their way back to the shore Zhuang Zhou had just left. As the two of them dried themselves in the sun, Zhuang Zhou spoke to the horse:

"I realize now that some beasts have a better sense of loyalty and self-sacrifice than many humans. I am quite content to have you and your master the old fisherman as my only friends in all the wide world."

He went on, after a heavy pause:

"But your mission and service to me at this stage of my life are completed. It is time for you to return to the old fisherman."

He thereupon wrote a brief note, attached it to the horse's mane, and sent the horse on its way.

The horse seemed to understand what he said, and set off northward at a leisurely trot.

After a few days, Zhuang Zhou came to the hinterland of the State of Chu (the area of the present-day provinces of Hubei and Hunan) between the Yuanshui and Xiangjiang rivers. He found himself in an enchanting wonderland, and wandered as if in a dream amid lofty mountains, graceful rivers, groves of willow trees and bamboos and carpets of bright flowers. Sometimes he would float aimlessly in a small boat on a stream or mirror-like lake; sometimes he would travel on foot in the lonely mountains; and sometimes he would visit quiet villages. Wherever he went, he found the countryside of Chu refreshing, lovely and exciting. He was intoxicated, infatuated even. He smiled at the flowers, stared at the clouds and mountains for hours, called to the singing birds and talked to the fish in the brooks.

The local people soon welcomed this stranger from the Central Plain, who was so unlike the greedy, grasping merchants from those parts they disliked so much. Weaving women, fishermen, hunters and farmers all treated him kindly, and were eager to have him as a guest in their homes. They were thirsty for news about the Central Plain, the relations between the other states, and the new schools of philosophy they had vaguely heard about. They never failed to invite Zhuang Zhou to their dragon boat races, sacrificial rites, demonstrations of fighting skills, hunting, antiphonal singing in the fields, fishing and moonlight parties.

Zhuang Zhou had not expected the State of Chu to be so rich and colorful. He was especially impressed by the neatness of the natural landscape and the spontaneity and freedom of the local people's lives. Every day, he was cleansed by freshness, purified by natural instincts and refined by the lack of anything artificial about the place. He felt like a stranded fish that had found its way back to its native lake.

One day, Zhuang Zhou wandered into a dense patch of fruit trees. Large clusters of bananas were within the reach of anyone's hands. Coconuts clustered at the tops of some trees, peering at him like the heads of naughty boys. There were many fruits the names of which were unknown to him. Zhuang Zhou had been an expert tree climber from his boyhood, and he swarmed up one tree from which hung fruits like pearls and agates. He picked one, and tasted it. It was sour and astringent. He spat it out. He then clambered up another tree, which bore fruits looking like something between a peach and an apricot. He ate one, finding it very sweet. Suddenly, he felt drowsy. Alighting from the tree, he wandered on until he came to a large banyan tree. There, he stretched himself on the grass and fell asleep.

In a dream, he saw a pair of peacocks approaching him. They allowed him to caress them. Truly Chu was the land of supreme virtue described by the old fisherman! How friendly and harmonious was the relationship between man and man, and between man and bird and beast was! And how different from the Central Plain, where deceit, killing and looting reigned!

The most unforgettable thing for Zhuang Zhou during his sojourn in Chu was his attendance at a grand sacrificial rite.

The rite started at dawn one crisp autumn morning.

Zhuang Zhou noticed that there was no strict separation of the people, or of the sexes or ages as in the Central Plain. To a flat and grassy plain crowds of people flocked from all directions. They chatted and laughed — men and women, old and young, jostled each other, standing or sitting just as they pleased. Young men and women crowded together, teasing each other freely. The seniors also talked and laughed happily to their hearts' content under the blue sky and surrounded by the mountain forests. Children played, little girls and boys rolling together on the grass. The young ladies were colorfully dressed, with bright flowers decorating them, as if to attract the attention of the young men. Some people were dressed in their best clothes, some still wore their work clothes, and some were even naked to the waist. They all formed a crude circle, some sitting in nearby trees and some standing on mounds to get a better view of the proceedings. There was no difference between the eminent and the humble.

The throng fell silent as a drum sounded. Zhuang Zhou squeezed to the front of the crowd, and asked an old man which deity was to be honored by the sacrifice.

"Taiyi, the Eastern Emperor," was the reply. "He is the chief of all the gods of the Chu people. He is partial to fish and to pretty women."

A cry drew their attention to the center of the circle, where an altar had been erected.

The high priest, in ceremonial robe and a tall hat, held aloft a glittering sword. The altar was built of bamboo and decorated with fresh flowers of all the colors of the rainbow. On the altar were heaped the five cereals, fruits of all imaginable descriptions and cooked food, including luscious fish dishes, as offerings to the god. In the center of the offerings was a beautiful young girl and a sturdy bamboo embellished with pearls and gems.

To the one side of the altar was a huge suspended drum of the Chu type, with two red-clad drummers standing by. The drum was supported by two brightly colored images of phoenixes (a male and a female), one standing on a tiger and the other on a lion.

The sword in the hand of the high priest rose and fell slowly three times. Thereupon, an orchestra behind the altar struck up a solemn air. Zhuang Zhou was struck by the oddity of the ritual musical instruments: The stringed and percussion instruments were of types he had never seen before. Some of the musicians were beating on bamboo tubes, and others were even producing high-pitched sounds from tree leaves. The high priest, brandishing his sword, began to dance. As he did so, he sang:

On this auspicious day, we await Our Lord,
With golden brilliance, the long sword shines in my hand.
Wearing jade rings, we are in high spirits,
The instruments of stone and metal clamor.

The drummers beat the giant drum furiously. The high priest raised a cup of wine, whereupon a bevy of bewitching girls appeared, dressed in thin gauze which showed the outlines of their slender bodies. Waving their long sleeves, the girls sang a cheerful song and danced gracefully.

Zhuang Zhou thought to himself: "The senior god of the Chu people, the Eastern Emperor Taiyi, is no hypocrite, not like the disguised and veiled deities of the Central Plain." The girls sang:

When the sticks are raised,
The drums sound.
When the flute is played,
The bamboo strains are heard.
When the wind and strings are played,
The singing is loud and clear.
When we are dancing,
The clouds are floating.
When the flowers are in bloom,
Fragrance spreads all around.
When the god comes,
The crowds sing in his praise.

Suddenly, the people burst into loud applause and cheers, as a figure dressed as the Eastern Emperor Taiyi sprang up in the center of the altar. He joined the girls in singing a hymn for good fortune, the safety of the people and bumper harvests.

Then the whole crowd of people joined in the dancing and singing, dragging Zhuang Zhou with them.

76

Whether it was something about Zhuang Zhou's appearance that marked him off as a stranger or his awkward attempts to imitate the local dancing style, he nevertheless attracted the attention of the man who was impersonating the god, the Eastern Emperor Taiyi.

Zhuang Zhou's heart thumped in his chest as the deity approached, with a humorously quizzical gleam in his eyes. He bowed his head in reverence. He felt the divine hand touching him lightly on the crown, and all of a sudden a great cheer erupted from the worshippers. Zhuang Zhou was hoisted shoulder-high, as flowers were showered over his head and a garland was heaped round his neck. Some uncanny force opened his lips, and from them came forth a paean to the god Taiyi:

The Eastern Emperor brings the morning light,
The myriad things grow sturdily, refreshed by the beams.
Exceedingly beautiful is the land of Chu,
And how transported with delight am I, a man from the north!

The Boisterous State of Yue

Zhuang Zhou came to the conclusion that the old fisherman had been right: The State of Chu was a world of supreme virtue. In particular, he could never forget the scene of the grand sacrificial rite.

Zhuang Zhou lingered in Chu for one whole year, and then reminded himself that his original intention was to see and experience as much as he could of the local conditions and customs in different places. Therefore, he bade farewell to his friends in Chu, and set off further down the Yangtze River to visit the State of Yue, which was located in the area of the present-day provinces of Zhejiang and Jiangsu.

The great river was an awesome sight as it flowed eastward with great rolling waves. Zhuang Zhou hired a small boat, which the old boatman did not have to row, but simply use the rudder to adjust the direction and let the current do the rest.

Zhuang Zhou stood at the bow gazing round

at the superb landscape, reviewing the villages, woods and mountain ridges, and the few carriages, horses and travelers to be spied on the banks. It was summer with refreshing breezes and pleasant temperature. He was feeling in an uplifted mood, as if he had at last found the land of the harmonious Tao, when something happened to awaken him rudely from this illusion.

He hardly noticed another boat passing close by, until he heard a splash. Startled, Zhuang Zhou jerked his head round, and saw a young girl struggling in the water. She had evidently fallen from the other boat, but the four other occupants of that vessel seemed completely unconcerned with the girl's plight, as was the boatmen.

The benign impression Zhuang Zhou had had of the people of the south vanished like a puff of smoke.

"What barbarians!" he muttered through gritted teeth, as he dived into the water to rescue the girl. Zhuang Zhou had become a powerful swimmer after many summers swimming in Mengze Lake, and it did not take him long to reach the girl and pull her into his own boat.

In the meantime, the four young men, who had seemed so indifferent to the accident, had also plunged into the river and swum toward the girl. But they were too late, and had to content themselves with treading water, scowls on their faces.

Zhuang Zhou's boatman laughed, and said, "Congratulations, young man! It was a stroke of luck for you, taking my boat. Now you have won yourself a beautiful bride!"

Zhuang Zhou could make neither head nor tail of this strange situation, until the boatman explained.

"It's the custom in these parts," he said, "for rivals for the hand of a beautiful girl to take her onto the river, and throw her in the water. They then swim after her, and the first one to reach her claims her as his bride. So you now have a wife!"

Zhuang Zhou was flabbergasted. Hastily explaining that he was from the north, and unaware of the customs of Yue, he declined his prize. The four young men showed themselves very understanding, not surprisingly, and agreed to relieve Zhuang Zhou of his unexpected burden.

As he penetrated deeper into Yue territory, Zhuang Zhou changed to traveling by land. On his way, he made the acquaintance of a trader from his home state of Song, called Wan Fu. After having had to strain his ears for more than a year to understand the strange dialect of the Chu people, he found it particularly cordial to converse freely in the Song dialect once more.

Wan Fu and his assistants had brought a load of hats to sell in Yue, but no matter in which market they set up their stall, they had no sales for many days. Clothing did not seem high on the list of priorities of the people of Yue, some of whom dressed only in animal skins. Tattoos were common, giving them a rather coarse and wild appearance. Eventually, Wan Fu managed to persuade a man of seemingly superior status to try on a hat. The first one he tried on was too tight. He then tried several others, but they were all too tight. Finally, he threw Wan Fu some money, and took a hat.

"It's no good as a hat," he said, nonchalantly, "but I can use it as a piss-pot."

With a guffaw, he tossed the hat into the gaping crowd, and stalked off.

Wan Fu was livid at this coarse behavior, muttering that people here had no sense of what was proper and it was obvious that Confucius had never visited the place. But Zhuang Zhou found it very amusing. The people here were unwilling to subject themselves to restraint, he thought. They were free, and would not allow their heads to be made uncomfortable simply for the sake of empty fashion.

Wan Fu's dejection at the poor reception his hats were getting was suddenly lifted when he discovered that valuable animal furs and pelts could be purchased in large quantities in Yue at rock-bottom prices. Such items were in great demand in the Central Plain, and he saw his way to making a great profit.

Leaving Zhuang Zhou at the inn to look after his luggage and goods, Wan Fu took his assistants off to purchase furs and pelts.

Zhuang Zhou spent his time roaming about the hills and fields, drinking in the scenery of Yue and making new friends.

One evening, as he was taking a stroll, musing on the philosophical theory of the relationships between Heaven, Earth and Man, a young man emerged from a wood carrying several braces of pheasants he had just shot and humming a cheerful tune. As soon as he saw Zhuang Zhou, the young man stopped humming, and approached him.

"Sir, you are not one of those fur and skin traders, are you?" he asked.

"No. I'm not a trader. I've come specially to your state to see the sights," Zhuang Zhou replied.

"I thought not; you don't look like a trader," the lad said.

The two chatted, and the young hunter, whose name was Wu Tong, demonstrated his shooting skill by downing a distant sparrow with his catapult in the twinkling of an eye. He then insisted that Zhuang Zhou accompany him home to a pheasant dinner.

The house was of a type peculiar to this southern region. It was built of bamboo resting on wooden pilings. Covered with a thatched roof, the house was divided into bedrooms, a kitchen and a storeroom. It was very cosy, and had no walled courtyard like houses in the Central Plain. Groves of fruit trees, and clusters of flowers, trees, shrubs and green grass separated the houses in the vicinity. To Zhuang Zhou, it was a wonderfully natural arrangement.

Zhuang Zhou asked his new friend. "There is no wall around your house. Aren't you worried about thieves?"

Wu Tong answered, "Theft is unknown in our state. So we never lock our doors, even when there is no one to look after the house. In fact, we scarcely ever close our doors, as there is no reason to keep neighbors or visitors out."

Wu Tong then called out to his mother and his sister that they had a guest for supper.

Zhuang Zhou and Wu Tong were met at the top of the wooden steps leading up to the house by a woman and a girl in her teens.

The older woman was Wu Tong's mother. She

looked in her fifties. Her hair was graying, but not thin. It was worn in a high bun. She had bright eyes and quick movements. The girl was Wu Tong's sister. Her sharp eyes flashed, and she laughed from time to time. Dressed in a thin linen jacket, she followed her mother like a shadow, and greeted the guest from afar naturally and gracefully.

Zhuang Zhou, Wu Tong and the latter's mother sat on the floor, while Wu Tong's sister, Wu Ling, brought them glutinous rice cakes, bananas, papayas and rice wine.

After a while, Wu Tong said to Zhuang Zhou, "Please keep my mother company. My sister and I are going to cook the pheasant."

So saying, he took his sister by the hand, and led her into the kitchen.

Zhuang Zhou was amazed to learn that his new friend's mother was over 70 years old.

"How do you keep yourself so healthy and youthful-looking?" he asked.

"Here, we rise at dawn and work in the fields until dusk," she replied. "We have no worries; we just let Nature take its course. My husband was strong and healthy, too. He would be alive and working today, just like me, if it had not been for an attack of malaria which took him from us some years ago."

It occurred to Zhuang Zhou that although there is a limit to man's life, there is no limit to knowledge of the world. To seek the limitless while endowed only with a limited life, one would be bound to feel tired and puzzled. Therefore, a man must let Nature take its course just as this old lady did. Without many desires, one would not have many disappointments, nor many sorrows or worries. The internal and external surroundings would naturally be good, and man would live to his longest span.

Seeing Zhuang Zhou pondering, the old lady asked:

"Sir, what are you thinking about?"

Zhuang Zhou replied:

"What you've just said has inspired me greatly. People can preserve their lives and die a natural death only when they stand aloof from the world, have no worries and do things according to the law of Nature, like you. People in the Central Plain make desperate efforts to seek honor, position, wealth, money and long life. They wear themselves out in these fruitless pursuits."

At this point, Wu Tong and his sister brought in the cooked pheasant, and they all settled down to enjoy the feast, while chatting and joking.

In the midst of the merriment, a loud whistle was heard outside, followed by a snatch of song:

A bright moon rises above the hill,
Birds go off to dreamland in pairs.
Clusters of bananas hang on the trees,
I invite my younger sister to have a taste.

It was a young man's voice, and Wu Ling sprang to her feet as soon as she heard it. Tripping to the doorway, she answered with a song of her own:

Why should the bees hum in the evening?
Fresh flowers are in bud.
The bananas on the trees are still green,
Wait for autumn if you want to eat sweet fruit.

Then both she and the unknown young man burst into peals of laughter.

Wu Ling darted back to the table, picked a choice piece of pheasant breast, and ran outside with it.

Zhuang Zhou found that the people in Yue were simpler and more natural than those in the State of Chu. They scorned fancy clothes and ornaments. He reflected that the incident on the river and Wu Ling's words and actions would all be considered scandalous by the people of the Central Plain. There, marriages were arranged between families through the services of a match-maker. In many cases the bride and groom had not even seen each other before the actual wedding night. Such free and easy relations between lovers as he had just witnessed would be impossible in the areas where the so-called benevolence, justice, propriety, wisdom and truthfulness advocated by Confucius now prevailed.

Zhuang Zhou recalled Confucius' words: "Of all people, girls and servants are the most difficult to behave to. If you are familiar with them, they lose their humility. If you maintain a reserve toward them, they are discontented." Confucianism dictated that men and women should not allow their hands to touch when giving and receiving things. This hide-bound doctrine greatly restricted the freedom of the people, especially the freedom between young men and young women. It was the cause of many tragedies. Confucianism was a poisonous sword, he concluded. The concepts of propriety and justice were bonds that shackled the people. How happy, free and fortunate were the people of Yue!

When Zhuang Zhou thought of this, he asked Wu Tong with a smile:

"Does your sweetheart live near here?"

Wu Tong replied:

"She lives in the village on the other side of

the hill. I got to know her when I was hunting there. I'm going to meet her in the moonlight later."

Returning to his inn, Zhuang Zhou lay awake far into the night. He was impressed how the common people of Yue — hunters, farmers, old and young — were sincere, calm and happy, despite being mostly illiterate, knowing nothing of the etiquette and ceremonies of the Central Plain and being completely oblivious of the teachings of the sages. He felt that he wanted to live among them for a long time.

A few days later, Zhuang Zhou called on Wu Tong again. He found the young hunter, his mother and sister singing and dancing in the midst of a jubilant crowd. Approaching them, he asked Wu Tong what the occasion for such a celebration was.

Wu Tong replied:

"The father of my sister's sweetheart has died."

Nonplussed, Zhuang Zhou protested:

"But surely, that should call for mourning, not joy! Why are you singing and dancing?"

Wu Tong said:

"A man originally has no life. Who gives it to him? The gods do. Now the gods have taken that life back, and the old man has returned to Heaven, where he belongs. That is why we are rejoicing."

Thereupon, Wu Ling urged Zhuang Zhou to join them in congratulating the old man on his return to Heaven.

Zhuang Zhou did so. While he was dancing, with clumsy steps, he thought how stupid the people in the Central Plain were for being terrified by death and holding solemn funeral rites, with weeping and wailing. The people of the State of Yue regarded death as nothing more than the return of life to its original place, just like a stray child returning to his own home.

That evening, Zhuang Zhou took a stroll. Looking up at the sky, he noticed that the moon and stars over Yue were just the same as over Song, but the customs and view of life of the people of Yue made them full of vigor, relaxed, happy and carefree.

Visit to the State of Wei

His visit to Yue had provided Zhuang Zhou with a glimpse of a world where harmony between men themselves and between men and Nature was possible, under the rule of supreme virtue. He was seized with a desire to bring tidings of this happy land back to the Central Plain and his native State of Song.

A couple of weeks after he had attended the funeral service of her sweetheart's father, he received an invitation to Wu Ling's wedding. It came as a great surprise to him, as in the Central Plain not only were such frivolous activities as singing and dancing strictly forbidden in the family for several months after a parent's death, but the children had to remain in mourning for three years. Here, however, a young man was to celebrate his marriage only a week or two after the demise of his father!

The wedding ceremony itself was very simple. It was held at the same place where the funeral service had been held. The bride and the groom paid their respects to the mothers of the two families, and their thanks to the villagers and friends who had come to congratulate them. Then, they sang, danced and drank wine until late in the evening.

Zhuang Zhou, slightly tipsy, sang a nuptial song to the happy couple:

How beautiful the landscape of Yue is,
How exhilarating the ways of its people!
Drain a bowl of sweet wine at one gulp,
And make a wish for the lovebirds to always
    fly in happiness.

The following day, Zhuang Zhou left the district with Wan Fu's caravan on their journey back to the north.

Wan Fu traveled slowly, making purchases of the local products on the way. Thus, Zhuang Zhou had plenty of time for more sightseeing in Yue, and for contemplating what he had seen and heard there.

They arrived back in Song the following spring. It had been three full years since he had left home. Zhuang Zhou was shocked by how dreary Suiyang, the capital of Song, looked in contrast to the lively and prosperous cities of the south. He felt no inclination to linger in Suiyang, but hurried away, eager to see his home village and his aged mother.

As Mt. Mengshan and Mengze Lake came into sight, Zhuang Zhou found his eyes misting over. Tears of joy streamed down his face as he pushed open the door of his mother's humble cottage, and took the frail old lady in his arms. Mother looked much older than he had seen her three years before, her hair sprinkled with grey and her face streaked with wrinkles.

After dining with his mother and sister-in-law — for his brother was away on a business trip to Suiyang and his nephew had not yet been home from school, Zhuang Zhou hastened to see the old fisherman by Mengze Lake. He was greeted by a neighing sound from the stable behind the old man's hut, and when he went to look, he was delighted to see his faithful companion, the horse the fisherman had given him!

As he was feeding the horse some tender shoots of grass and stroking its neck affectionately, the old fisherman appeared, with his fishing pole over his shoulder and his fish basket in his hand. As he approached, he sang:

I heard the magpie chirp,
And so I knew I have a guest.
My horse neighed,

As a fish jumped at the bait.
The emperor is far from shining Mengze Lake,
I take my small boat in the sunset glow.
Others shun the fisherman,
But there's a close friend who knows me truly.

The old man was eager to hear all about his young friend's sojourn in the south. The two chatted and chatted about the wonders of the states of Chu and Yue until the sky was studded with stars, when the fisherman poled Zhuang Zhou across the lake in his boat.

At dawn the next day, Zhuang Zhou was wakened with rough good humor by his brother, who wanted to question him about his travels. Zhuang Yan, his cheeks now filled out although his hairline receding, remarked that his younger brother was looking gaunt and under-fed.

"Traveling doesn't seem to agree with you," he said. "You should settle down here from now on, and stop wandering. We have a whole hectare of land, and I don't have the time to take care of it. Besides, you are nearly 30; it's time you got married. When you were away, mother was always talking about it."

Zhuang Zhou seemed not to have heard what his brother had said; at any rate, he changed the subject abruptly:

"I heard that my good friend Hui Shi is a high official in the State of Wei these days....By the way, how is Hui Ze?"

Zhuang Yan said, "Hui Ze has not gone anywhere. He is married, and they have a baby."

Zhuang Zhou sighed, "It comes as no surprise to me."

A few days later, just as he had done three springs previously, Zhuang Zhou bade farewell again to his mother, brother and sister-in-law, and then to the old fisherman, and left for the State of Wei to visit Hui Shi. But this time, he had no horse to ride, and he was journeying north instead of south.

He had not gone far, when he fell in with Su Yu, whom he knew by sight as a former pupil at the Mt. Mengshan school. The latter was younger than Zhuang Zhou, and was an idle scoundrel who had learned little at school and shown a talent for nothing but gambling and carousing. Zhuang Zhou knew nothing of Su Yu's reputation, and replied cordiality to Su Yu's effusive greeting:

"Mr. Zhuang, I heard that you have greatly increased your learning during your three years of travel in the south. A man of your erudition surely has a brilliant official career ahead of him! You are perhaps on your way at this moment to call on the ruler of our illustrious state?"

"No, actually, I am bound for Daliang, the capital of the State of Wei."

"Oh, I see. I heard that your good friend Hui Shi is now the prime minister of Wei. Well then, with his assistance a senior post there will be yours for the asking no doubt."

"Not at all," said Zhuang Zhou, emphatically. "Hui Shi and I have different political views. Officialdom is not for me."

This gave the crafty Su Yu an idea. "Aha!" he thought to himself, "this Zhuang Zhou is such a simpleton that he doesn't know that a slip of the tongue like that could cost him his head!"

In no time at all, he had formed a plan to speed ahead of Zhuang Zhou to Daliang and ingratiate himself with Hui Shi by claiming that Zhuang Zhou was coming to make trouble for him.

With an excuse, and cloying expressions of good will, Su Yu parted from Zhuang Zhou, and hurried day and night by little-used roads to Daliang.

At this time, Hui Shi was in the midst of negotiations with Chunyu Kun, an envoy from the State of Qi. Hui Shi had persuaded King Hui of Wei that it was in his state's best interest to form a pact with Qi, despite Wei's humiliating defeat some years before at the hands of Qi at the Battle of Guiling. Chunyu Kun was renowned throughout all the states for his wisdom and austerity. He came from a humble family, and lived in the house of his wife's parents. His children were brought up as part of his wife's family.

The reign of King Xuan's predecessor, King Wei of the State of Qi had got off to an unpropitious start. King Wei seemed to care for nothing but wine, women and song, and as no one at court had the courage to admonish him, the state seemed set for ruin. Chunyu Kun, however, got his master to mend his ways by telling him a parable, which went as follows:

"There is a large bird in the State of Qi. It nests in the court of Your Majesty. It has not yet flown or uttered a cry for three years. Do you know what that bird is, Your Majesty?"

The king grasped the allusion immediately.

"You mean the roc!" he cried. "The mythical bird which takes to flight but once, and when it does so it soars into the very heavens. Moreover, it utters only one cry, but this cry astounds the whole universe."

From then on, King Wei turned over a new leaf, diligently attending to state affairs and encouraging the airing of views and criticisms. He went so far as to issue a decree:

"Anyone who criticizes me to my face shall receive the top state award; anyone who presents a written admonition shall receive the medium state prize; and anyone who raises a criticism in a public place shall receive a third-class state award."

Before long, the State of Qi took its place in the ranks of the seven strongest states of the Warring States Period.

Having persuaded the gate guard at Hui Shi's mansion that he was the prime minister's old schoolmate, Su Yu was led into Hui Shi's presence.

Hui Shi only vaguely remembered Su Yu, who was about a dozen years his junior, but he still welcomed him courteously, and after exchanging the usual pleasantries asked him the purpose of his visit.

Su Yu leaned forward, with an air of solemn mystery, and whispered:

"Sir, I have come to warn you of danger approaching. Someone intends to try to oust you from your post and make himself prime minister of Wei."

"Who?" cried Hui Shi in alarm and puzzlement.

"Nobody else but your old companion Zhuang Zhou!"

"Zhuang Zhou? The last I heard, he had gone to the south."

"Well, sir, he is back now, boasting that he had learned magical arts of statecraft from the wizards of the states of Chu and Yue. What's more, he is on his way here at this very moment, confident that he will win the ear of King Hui, replace you as prime minister, and put into practice his heretical ideas about government."

Hui Shi protested, "Oh no! I know Zhuang Zhou well; he would never serve princes and dukes, much less wish to become prime minister."

Nevertheless, he knew that if Zhuang Zhou really did come to Wei he must prevent him from having an audience with the king at all costs. In this, he was spurred by his affection for his old friend: Zhuang Zhou was so outspoken and contemptuous of protocol that he might easily rouse the king's anger.

He gave orders for lodgings to be found for Su Yu, and went out into his garden to ponder what he had been told.

In the garden, the peach blossoms were as pink as the morning glow, the crabapple trees shone green and silvery, the pear blossoms were as white as snow, the winter jasmine looked like gold necklaces and the Chinese redbud was like a tree of burning torches. They were intermingled with apricot blossoms, roses, and papaya blooms, forming a veritable sea of flowers. However, on this day Hui Shi scarcely noticed them — he was too busy racking his brains trying to think of a way to prevent Zhuang Zhou getting access to the court of Wei without arousing suspicion about his motives.

He was on the point of despair, when an aide approached him and asked for his authorization to circulate a wanted poster for a notorious bandit.

"That's it!" cried the exultant Hui Shi. "That's the way I'll do it!"

He then dispatched the puzzled aide for writing materials, and made a copy of the wanted poster. But this one was for the arrest of a certain Zhuang Zhou, a suspected assassin no less!

That done, he gave orders for the two wanted posters to be pasted up both inside and outside the city of Daliang.

Zhuang Zhou Lectures King Hui of Wei

Daliang (located northwest of present-day Kaifeng City in Henan Province) was the newly built capital of the State of Wei. Soldiers carrying halberds were on constant patrol on the parapets of the lofty city wall, which overlooked a moat a dozen meters wide.

Zhuang Zhou joined the crowd which was jostling its way through the main gate of the city across a broad drawbridge. His attention was drawn to a knot of people gazing at two posters pasted up on the wall of the city entrance. He too stopped to read the posters, and was thunderstruck to see that one of them offered a reward of 50 taels of silver for his arrest as a suspected assassin! There was a likeness of him painted quite accurately on the poster, which bore the seal of the prime minister himself.

Not daring to enter the city now, Zhuang Zhou hurried back the way he had come, put up at a small roadside inn, and lay down on his bed to try to solve this monstrous riddle.

What really puzzled him was how Hui Shi could have learned that he was on his way to Wei, not to mention how his old friend could have accused him of harboring criminal intentions. No doubt the kind-hearted and innocent Hui Shi of old had been corrupted by power and wealth, which had warped his perceptions so much that he could not bear the thought of a rival, even if that rival had once been his bosom companion.

Just then, he remembered the other poster. It had been for the arrest of a bandit chief, hadn't it? Bandits, he reflected, took what they, their relatives, fellow workers or the like had created and should have belonged to them. Rather than hunt such people down, the righteous should first arrest and put to death those princes and dukes who usurped state power and stole the people's wealth while bringing misery to the land with fire and sword. He recalled how Tian Chengzi slew Duke Kang of Qi and made himself the ruler of that state, in the name of "benevolence and justice."

He recalled his ghostly conversation with the skull on that dreary battlefield during his trip to the south, and this strengthened his resolve to confront Hui Shi, come what may.

The following morning, as Zhuang Zhou strode boldly through the city gate a ragged urchin clutched at him, and begged for the price of a meal for his mother and himself. Zhuang Zhou's pockets were empty, and he was just about to apologize for being unable to help him, when an idea struck him.

"Follow me, boy," he said, "and I'll get 50 taels of silver for you."

"Fifty taels?" the boy cried in incredulity. "Oh sir, please do not mock a poor beggar. My mother and I have not eaten for two days; a few coppers would be enough."

"I don't have even a few coppers," replied Zhuang Zhou, "but if you do what I say, I will provide you with 50 taels of silver." As he said this, he pointed to the wanted poster.

The boy gave a shudder of fear, as he realized that he was talking to a desperate assassin. He asked in surprise: "Sir, are you not afraid of being beheaded?"

"No. Good fortune and bad visit us in turns, and come in their own time. There is no escaping either."

Then, casting around, Zhuang Zhou found a piece of discarded rope, which he instructed the boy to tie his hands with.

The guards at the gate of the prime minister's mansion roared with laughter when they saw a skinny boy leading a grown man at the end of a piece of rope. When the lad claimed to have captured the assassin Zhuang Zhou, they thought he was playing a game with them, and tried to shoo him away. But when his captive claimed to be the real Zhuang Zhou and demanded to be led to the prime minister for identification, the guards looked him up and down first, then reluctantly complied.

Hui Shi did not wait for the strange pair to be admitted to his presence, but hurried to the gate himself.

He recognized Zhuang Zhou at once, although he noticed that his complexion was somewhat darker, and he seemed more poised and mature.

Hui Shi personally untied Zhuang Zhou's hands, and was about to lead him inside, apologizing profusely for what now seemed to have been a gross error of judgment.

Zhuang Zhou hesitated.

"First, I have a promise to keep," he said, and explained how he had promised the beggar boy 50 taels of silver.

Hui Shi abruptly ordered an aide to fetch 50 tales of silver, give them to the happy boy and escort him home with his little fortune. After he saw this done, Zhuang Zhou accompanied his old friend into the mansion.

When they were seated in the prime minister's study, Zhuang Zhou said:

"I gave myself up to you today, instead of fleeing, to find out why you, my old classmate, fear me so much. But before you decide what to do with me, I would like to tell you a story."

Then, without more ado, he launched into his tale:

"There is a bird called the phoenix in the south of China. It once made a journey from the South Sea to the North Sea. On its way, it did not perch on any other tree but the parasol tree, nor did it eat any other fruit than that of the bamboo, or drink other than pure and sweet spring water, because it feared that other things would sully its noble and clean body. One day, a sparrow hawk was pecking at a stinking dead mouse, when it looked up and saw the phoenix flying from the south. Thinking that the phoenix would steal its prey, the sparrow hawk glared at it and shrieked to frighten it away."

Hui Shi burst out laughing at this:

"My dear Zhuang Zhou, you've made great progress in eloquence. However, this is just a small misunderstanding. I'm not the kind of sparrow hawk which is greedy for a dead mouse!"

He then told his visitor of Su Yu's treachery.

The two old friends chatted over dinner late into the night. Hui Shi insisted that Zhuang Zhou stay with him, and the two spent many happy hours together in the following days.

One evening, Hui Shi returned home in a state of great excitements.

"King Hui has heard of your coming, and wants you to call on him tomorrow," he told Zhuang Zhou.

At first Zhuang Zhou was reluctant.

"I don't think there's any need for me to have an audience with the king, as I don't seek any preferment or official post," he said.

But after much persuasion from the prime minister, Zhuang Zhou finally agreed. However, one thing he was adamant about was that he appear before the king wearing his travel-stained hemp clothes and straw sandals. With a sigh, Hui Shi reluctantly agreed, but added a word of advice:

"The king is advanced in years and a kindly-looking man. But if he is angered, he can be as fierce as a tiger. You must be careful what you say to him."

On the following day, Hui Shi and Zhuang Zhou took the prime minister's carriage, and arrived at the royal palace at the appointed time.

When they were ushered into the presence of King Hui, Hui Shi kowtowed, and then took a seat on the right of the king. Zhuang Zhou, however, stood looking around at the magnificent furnishings in the hall.

An attendant shouted to Zhuang Zhou to kowtow to the ruler of Wei, but Zhuang Zhou simply replied:

"I am not a subject of the ruler of Wei; why should I perform an obeisance to him?"

King Hui was not perturbed at this commotion, and simply said:

"Your reputation for informality is well deserved, I see. Come forward, and let my dim old eyes have a good look at you."

But Zhuang Zhou did not budge. He said:

"According to Lao Zi, 'Although you are eminent, you must take the humble as the foundation. Although you are above, you must take what is below as the foundation.' So if you regard yourself as eminent, you should humble yourself, showing that you are courteous to the wise and benign to the scholarly. If I were to go to you, wouldn't that mean that I would be toadying to a man of influence?"

While Hui Shi looked on, horrified, the king slowly rose from his throne, approached Zhuang Zhou, and inspected him with curiosity. Finally, the king asked:

"You surpass others in wisdom and ability, why are you so shabbily dressed?"

Zhuang Zhou replied:

"Your Majesty, I'm poor and virtuous, but not shabby. If a scholar has no ideal to pursue, no spiritual pillar to support him, then he can be truly called shabby. A man like me, clothed in rags and with empty pockets can be said to be poor. But in my search for virtue, I am rich in my heart."

The king of Wei asked:

"Since your heart is abundant, why have you been reduced to this poor and pitiful condition?"

Zhuang Zhou replied:

"My poverty was not brought about by myself, but by wars and political upheavals. Has Your Majesty not seen the monkeys running and leaping to and fro? When they are in such trees as the nanmu, Chinese catalpa, elm and camphor and clamber over the smooth branches, they live freely and in boundless joy. They move as quickly as lightning, and even master archers can scarcely hit them. But when they come across the cudrania, thorn bush, orange tree and Chinese holly, they walk carefully, with their eyes carefully observing the surrounding branches and twigs. Any movement will make them palpitate with anxiety and fear. Why?

"It is because the surroundings are unfavorable to their movement. Now, in the age we live in, kings and princes are ambitious, fatuous and incompetent, while their officials all use their power solely to seek selfish interests and are blinded by greed, far surpassing the thorn bushes which the monkeys so fear. The people have lost the pillars they depended upon for life and are completely exhausted. There are too few people like me who seek spiritual ideals in poverty."

These words cut King Hui to the quick, but, realizing that this was not the moment to express his anger, he returned to his throne without saying a word. Such blunt talk and straightforward behavior had never been heard or seen in the palace before, and the hall had fallen eerily quiet. Hui Shi found that he could hear his own heartbeat. Zhuang Zhou, however, stood in the center of the hall, his head held high and seemingly oblivious to everybody else present. He was indeed in the realm of the void, where all was stillness.

King Hui felt that an exhilarating challenge had come his way. The old spark of combat and victory was rekindled in his old breast, and he said:

"Zhuang Zhou, I'm not one of the fatuous rulers you have described, nor is Hui Shi one of those shameless officials. I am prepared to allow you to live here in the State of Wei, like a monkey in the elm and camphor woods, if you wish."

Zhuang Zhou replied:

"Your Majesty, it was not to beg for your hospitality that I came to the State of Wei, but to bring you benefit at the request of my good classmate and friend."

At this, King Hui roared with laughter:

"As the ruler of a state with ten thousand chariots at my command, I have everything I could desire. How can you, a poor scholar, do anything to benefit me?"

"Your Majesty has indeed everything you could desire — and that is precisely why you are poor and unhappy," replied Zhuang Zhou.

The king started in astonishment. But before he could object, Zhuang Zhou continued:

"Satisfying your desires and whims with the sensual pleasures is a sure way to undermine the health. On the other hand, by eschewing all worldly pleasures, you deprive your body of what it craves. I will tell you of a way to avoid both disasters."

These words struck a chord in King Hui's heart. He had been in power for nearly 30 years, and all that time he had never ceased to scheme how to expand his territory and wealth, and stock his palace with beautiful women, mellow wine, and champion hunting dogs and horses. The result, he knew, had been unending anxiety. But he could not bear the thought of life without such things. Fascinated, he signaled for Zhuang Zhou to continue.

He did so: "Your Majesty, since you are very familiar with fine dogs and horses, let me talk about my standards for appraising them. The lowest-grade dogs know only how to go to sleep after filling their bellies; the medium-grade dogs are clever and alert, and bark at the sun; and the top-grade dogs look around superficially as if they have lost their souls, and do nothing.

"I appraise a horse in the same way. A superb horse walks as straight as a carpenter's line, circles in a perfect arc, and paces out an ideal rectangle. But there is an even better horse. This one relies on its natural qualities. It needs no training. At ordinary times, it looks listless, as if it has lost its soul. But once it begins to run, it runs as if soaring in freedom like a flying horse, leaving no trace and going no one knows whither."

King Hui shuffled in his seat.

"It is true, as you say, that top-grade dogs and horses look superficially listless," he nodded, "but what has that to do with me?"

Zhuang Zhou replied:

"My Lord, it has a lot to do with you! Don't you understand? If you can take good care of your natural instincts, get rid of the evil desires in your heart and let nature take its course, you can cure your ailments for good, just like a top-grade horse or dog."

The king looked pleased with this. He said:

"You are most persuasive, and I think I would like further instruction from you. You may stay here in the palace as my personal health attendant."

But to his amazement Zhuang Zhou was not at all impressed by this offer.

"Your Majesty," the philosopher said, "my form is like the cloud in the sky or the smoke from the ground; how can you make me fast? My body is like the wave in the river or the falling snow; how can it stay longer? My heart is like the blue sky or the yellow earth; how can you contain me? My formula for curing illnesses lies among the words you heard just now. I can't stay here in your state, even less can I look after you. I'm going to the mountains and wilderness to live a life free of cares."

With that, he bade Duke Hui farewell.

The flustered Hui Shi made a perfunctory kowtow to his ruler, and hurried after his friend.

An Unforgettable Meeting

To Zhuang Zhou, the most rejoicing, gratifying and unforgettable thing during his stay in Daliang was his meeting with Chunyu Kun, the envoy from the State of Qi. He had long known of the latter's illustrious reputation as a great thinker and statesman, and it was with a great sense of anticipation one bright spring day that he accompanied Hui Shi to a riverside meadow east of the city.

Chunyu Kun arrived in a sumptuous carriage. He was a tall man, with bushy whiskers and deeply sunken eyes shining with a brilliant light and shaded by slanting eyebrows. But despite his impressive appearance and fine clothes, Chunyu Kun proved to be a straightforward and friendly man, whose main interests were scholarly. When the introductions were over, he lost no time urging Zhuang Zhou and Hui Shi to be seated on a mat on the grass, and introduced his thoughts about the philosopher Mencius:

"There is not much difference in age between

Mencius and me. Mencius inherited Confucius's theory, and has had a big influence in Qi. He and I are opponents in argument, but we are also friends, because some of his views are correct. For example, he says that 'The people are the most important element in a nation; the state is the next; and the sovereign is of the least import.'

"These are the correct relations among the people, the state and the sovereign. However, the sovereign often thinks that he is pre-eminent and above everything else, while the people are subservient and completely at his mercy. However, many views of Mencius' are the same as those of Confucius, and are mere pedantry."

Hui Shi then told Zhuang Zhou how he and Chunyu Kun had been working together to try to ensure peace between their respective states.

"As an example of Chunyu Kun's penetrating insight, let me relate the episode of his first meeting with my master, King Hui. At their first interview, the king was absent-minded. Chunyu Kun perceived this, and said, 'Since Your Majesty has something else on your mind, let's talk another day.'

"At the next meeting, he said, 'Since Your Majesty is happy about something today and you are distracted, perhaps we should postpone our talk yet again?' After Chunyu Kun left, the king remarked to me: 'That Chunyu Kun is a man of great perspicacity! The first time I granted him an interview, I was still thinking about a magnificent horse somebody had presented me with, and I was absent-minded. On the second occasion, someone had recommended a fine singer to me. Again, I could not concentrate on the interview, and again I was unable to hide this from Chunyu Kun's sharp eyes.' At my suggestion, the king paid a special visit to Chunyu Kun. The two talked for three days and three nights. Even I was not permitted to be present."

In the bright spring sunshine, amid the buzzing of bees and chirping of birds, the three men — Hui Shi, Zhuang Zhou and Chunyu Kun — all with similar backgrounds, keen minds and academic interests delved deeply into a philosophical discourse. The only difference between them was that Hui Shi and Chunyu Kun were exalted officials, while Zhuang Zhou was a poor wandering scholar.

Hui Shi said:

"The king once gave me the seed of a bottle gourd. I sowed it. When it grew and ripened, it weighed 300 kilograms. When I hollowed it out and used it to hold water, it was too heavy to lift. Then I cut it in two to make two ladles. But they were far too big. In the end I decided that the

gourd was too big to be useful for anything, so I chopped it into pieces."

Zhuang Zhou answered this with a parable:

"Once upon a time, there was a man in the State of Song who had a secret recipe for an ointment to cure chapped hands. Hearing about this, a stranger from another state wanted to buy his prescription at a good price. The man of Song called a family meeting and said, 'For generations we have been eking out a living by rinsing used cotton fiber. Now we have the chance to sell our secret prescription and live more comfortably.' The family agreed. Although they lived more comfortably than before by selling the prescription, they had to live on rinsing used cotton fiber in the long run. After getting the prescription, the stranger presented it to the ruler of the State of Wu. It was at a time when Wu was fighting a war with the State of Yue. Because Wu used the anti-chap drug, the morale of its troops was high, and they inflicted a crushing defeat on the Yue army. The ruler of Wu appointed the stranger who had presented him with the anti-chap prescription a senior official.

"You see, Hui Shi, the effect of the anti-chap drug was the same. However, the first possessor of it was unable to use it to lift himself far from poverty, while the second possessor became a senior official. Isn't this different from the case of your bottle gourd?"

After hearing this story, Chunyu Kun looked at the clear flowing water, and said with emotion:

"Four years ago, the State of Chu invaded Qi. My master, King Wei of Qi, sent me to the State of Zhao to ask for help, and gave me 50 kilograms of gold and ten chariots each drawn by four horses. I laughed sardonically. I laughed in such a way that my hat fell to the ground.

"When King Wei, baffled, asked me what I was laughing at, I told him the following anecdote: Once I saw a farmer praying for a bumper harvest in the fields. His offerings to the gods consisted of merely a piece of pork and a cup of wine. I laughed, and when my attendants asked why, I said, 'The farmer is asking for a bumper harvest, but all he can offer in return is a scrap of pork and a drop of wine. Isn't that laughable?' The king then gave me twenty thousand taels of gold, ten pairs of white jade ornaments and one hundred chariots each drawn by four horses. I thereupon went to the State of Zhao. After examining the gifts, the duke of Zhao immediately commanded one hundred thousand crack troops and one thousand chariots to be sent to help Qi. When the news of this was brought to the ruler of Chu, he withdrew his troops overnight.

"King Wei of Qi hosted a banquet in my honor. At it, he asked me my capacity for wine. I answered that I could drink either one flagon and become drunk, or as many as ten flagons and not get drunk. Astonished, he asked me to explain.

"So I said, 'At a formal banquet, with guards and law officers standing around, and the royal censor present, I will restrict myself to one flagon, pretending that I am already tipsy after that small amount. The reason is that I am afraid that a slip of the tongue could cost me my head. If I am ordered to accompany a respected guest in drinking, I can stand on less ceremony, and then two flagons is my limit. But if I meet friends after a long separation, and we chat quietly about the past, I can drink five or six flagons before getting drunk. If men and women sit together in a busy market tavern, drinking while playing the finger-guessing game, I can drink eight flagons and may get twenty percent drunk. When dinner is over and candles are lit, I will loosen my clothing and inhale some faint fragrance. I am in my best and most relaxed mood at this time, and can drink ten flagons. Therefore, the situations are different and the changes are great. Big or small, much or little exists by comparison. Both big and small have their respective advantages. Drinking is followed by loss of sobriety when it reaches its extreme, and happiness is followed by sorrow when it reaches its extreme. All things are guided by this principle. One should not exceed the limit and go in the opposite direction.'"

Hui Shi said:

"Indeed, that story is aimed at Zhuang Zhou here, for he has surely exceeded the limit with his lifestyle which eschews all worldly honors and wealth. I am afraid the common people will take no notice of his words. There is a large tree, called the 'Tree of Heaven.' Its trunk is so knotted that no line can be made by a carpenter's ink marker. It has small branches and twigs which are too crooked for the use of a carpenter's compass or square. Even if it were standing by the roadside, no carpenter would show interest in it."

Zhuang Zhou smiled and said:

"Hui Shi, haven't you seen the raccoon and wildcat? They skulk in hiding, waiting to catch passing birds and beasts. They leap here and there, at high or low places. They finally fall into the hunter's net.

"Now, you have a large tree, and you are worried over its uselessness. Then why don't you transplant it in a vast open country in a deserted region? You can pace up and down around it at leisure every day or lie under it carefree. It will not receive the blow of the axe, and nothing will hurt it. Since it is useless, how can it suffer hardships? King Hui of Wei found my remarks untenable, but they are practiced in real life in both Chu and Yue. Why?

"Just because the places are different, the people are different, and the situations are different. It is just like Mr. Chunyu's wine drinking. He gets drunk on one flagon, but can drink lots more without getting drunk."

Hui Shi nodded his agreement. Zhuang Zhou went on:

"People in different places have different customs and beliefs. When I was in the State of Chu I found that the people there believed they were the descendants of the God of the Sun and the God of Fire. Both the sun and fire are red, so the Chu people worship that color. They like all bright and heavy colors. Their robes, sleeves, silk goods and handicrafts are all decorated in bright colors. They are gorgeous, splendid and beautiful. People in the north worship the dragon, but the Chu people worship the phoenix."

Chunyu Kun told Hui Shi:

"It is really worth seeing the State of Chu. It has beautiful landscapes. It is full of life and vigor wherever you go. King Wei of Qi once sent me to Chu with some fine pigeons as a gift for the ruler of that state. However, the birds escaped before I got there. I told the ruler of Chu: 'My master wanted to give you some fine pigeons, but the pigeons were homesick and flew back home. So I thought it would be better to give myself to you instead. The pigeons can only coo, but I can talk with Your Majesty and tell you stories and handle matters for you. Am I much better than the pigeons?'

"He then asked for my advice. I said, 'If three people tend one sheep, the sheep will not eat and the shepherds will have no rest. Your Majesty should guard against this. This practice of three people tending one sheep used to be prevalent in the State of Qi, but it is now being abolished.' The ruler of Chu said, 'I know what you mean. When organizations are overstaffed, there are more hands than needed, administrative orders are issued from many departments, and there are more troops than civilians. In such a situation, how can a state be well governed? You are truly a man of deep thought.'"

In the State of Lu

Not long after Chunyu Kun departed for his home state, Zhuang Zhou informed Hui Shi that he too intended to leave the State of Wei. His friend was disappointed, but suggested that if he was determined to continue traveling he might join a diplomatic mission which was just about to leave Wei for the states of Lu and Zhao.

Zhuang Zhou accepted with alacrity.

A few days later, Zhuang Zhou bade farewell to Hui Shi and left Daliang with the diplomatic mission, journeying eastward. Along the way, he noticed that the crops were withering in the fields, and the dusty road was filled with wandering farmers, half-starved and clad in rags. Wistfully, Zhuang Zhou recalled the blue mountains and green waters in the prosperous states of Chu and Yue, the scene of the ritual, the blooming of the flowers and the singing of the birds, and the simple, friendly people he had met. Gazing again on the bare, dry and lifeless land and the desperate people, he felt dejected.

The mission eventually arrived at Qufu, the capital city of the State of Lu (located in the southwest of present-day Shandong Province). The following morning, Duke Jing of Lu paid a personal call on Zhuang Zhou at the state guest-house. The duke, who had newly come to the throne, had read Zhuang Zhou's article "Robber Zhi Denounces Confucius". Although he did not agree to Zhuang's views, he admired his imagination, skilful use of language and profound philosophy. He had also been impressed by reports of Zhuang Zhou's eccentric appearance and habits.

After exchanging a few words of greeting, the duke invited Zhuang Zhou to accompany him in his carriage to the palace.

When they were seated in the duke's private chamber, the latter said:

"We people of Lu are particularly proud of our most famous native son Confucius. During his lifetime, he traveled to many other states, but their rulers all turned a deaf ear to his teachings. Even here, he failed to obtain preferment. However, after his death, his teachings received universal acclaim, and now all scholars regard Confucianism as their guide."

"My Lord," replied Zhuang Zhou, "once Confucius was besieged by a great crowd of angry people. After seven days, he and his disciples began to run out of food, and faced the prospect of starvation. A local wise man named Tai Gong Ren went to see him, and asked, 'Are you afraid of death?' When Confucius replied in the affirmative, Tai Gong Ren said, 'Let me try to explain the principle of not dying. There is a bird in the region of the East Sea called Yidai. The bird flies very slowly as if it is very weak. It and its companions fly wing to wing, and crowd together for the night. When they advance, no one dares to take the lead. When they retreat, no one dares to lag behind. When they eat, no one dares to be the first to taste the food. They are bent on avoiding disasters and troubles. The straight timber is the first to be cut. The sweet well water is the first to be drained. Maybe you parade your knowledge to show up others' ignorance, and cultivate your body and soul to reveal others' shortcomings. If you do things in the brilliant light, it is like walking in the sun or moonlight. So you cannot avoid disasters and troubles. You have destroyed the simple and plain moral character of the common people. You ask them to seek benevolence, justice, propriety and wisdom, but you do so simply to win the favor of kings and princes, seeking fame and high rank. If you can, like the Yidai bird, abandon your self-consciousness, exist with the light and become one with the masses, you will find a way out of your impasse.'"

"Confucius thereupon sent away all his disciples and friends, and hid himself deep in the mountains. He wore hemp clothes and ate wild fruits. Both the birds and wild animals were on intimate terms with him. They never clashed, and no one came to oppose him."

As Zhuang Zhou finished this story, Duke Jing shook his head in bewilderment.

"I think you must have invented this tale," he protested. "All the scholars in Lu are followers of Confucian canon. They have collected all his words and remarks. I too am very familiar with Confucius' life, and I have never heard this anecdote about him."

Zhuang Zhou could not help laughing. He replied:

"My Lord, originally, there is anything or nothing in the world; there is nothing true or false. Making something out of nothing is the same as making the false true. Can you be sure that all the words of Confucius passed down by the scholars in Lu are true?

"On my way here, I saw many scholars in their fine robes, especially here in the city of Qufu. However, My Lord, please don't think that the wearers of round hats know the weather, that those wearing square-toed shoes know the physical features of the land, or that those wearing waist jades are skilled administrators. Do the Confucian teachings impart these qualities?"

The following morning, Zhuang Zhou was taking a stroll through the streets of Qufu when he saw a decree issued by Duke Jing pasted on the wall of the main gate of the city. A group of men in scholars' robes were perusing it carefully, and looking most disgruntled. When these men hurried away, muttering, Zhuang Zhou examined the decree, and found that it forbade the wearing of scholars' gowns and hats, upon pain of death. So Duke Jing had taken his words to heart after all!

In the afternoon, he took another stroll, and nowhere did he see a single person dressed as a scholar, not even at Xingtan, where Confucius taught his disciples.

On the following day, Duke Jing called on Zhuang Zhou at the guesthouse again. He asked him why Confucianism was something that was easily imitated but not inwardly digested. Zhuang Zhou said, with a smile:

"My Lord, Confucianism teaches benevolence, justice, propriety and wisdom. These things were formulated by your forefather the Duke of Zhou, and imposed on the common people. They do not come from the natural instincts of man, but instead go against them. Therefore, if the Confucian principles are used to rule a state, the state will surely perish. If the principles of Confucianism are applied to cultivate yourself, your moral culture is bound to collapse. However, the scholars of the Confucian school have regarded these dregs as gems. They have swindled and bluffed here and there to win favor from rulers so as to gain riches and rank. Such people may speak of benevolence, justice and virtue, but they behave like thieves and whores!"

The duke said:

"That is surely true. I have noticed that since the principles of Confucianism have been applied to rule Lu, the state's strength has been steadily declining. On the other hand, Qin is rising fast, Chu is glaring like a tiger eyeing its prey, Qi is planning to restore its hegemony and Wei is as ambitious as ever. The states of Chen, Cai, Yue and Zheng have all perished, while the states of Han, Wei and Zhao have divided up the State of Jin between them, and the Tian family has replaced the Jiang family in Qi. Wars among the states are never-ending, and the weak are the prey of the strong. In this situation, how can I free myself from worries and anxieties? Please give me your advice."

Zhuang Zhou replied:

"My Lord, you are right. The world's affairs, and the affairs of the State of Lu have indeed laden you with anxieties. If you want to get rid of them, it is not difficult for you to do so. Haven't you seen the beautiful fox and the spotted leopard? They dwell in the thickly forested mountains and hide in caves. You can't say that they do not like quietness. They hide during the day, and come out at night. You can't say that they are not careful. Driven by hunger and thirst, they get their food and drinking water from mountains and rivers afar. You can't say that they are not alert. However, they still can't escape the traps set by the hunters. Why?

"It is just because their furs and skins are too beautiful and bring disaster upon them. My Lord, the State of Lu is the fur and skin by which you've invited trouble and worry! Your neighbors are all plotting to seize your territory. If you persist in clinging to your throne, how can you be free from endless anxieties? If you can remove this layer of fur and skin from your body, and use the spiritual influence of nature to clear selfish desires from your mind and set your mind free to wander in the void, your anxieties and worries will all disappear."

"How can the mind be freed?" asked the duke.

"There is a place in the State of Yue called Jiande. The people there are simple, honest, selfless and free from desires. They work, but they do not know how to store. They grant things to others, but they do not seek reward from them. They know nothing of benevolence, justice, propriety and wisdom, but they live the most harmonious and best lives. They have no knowledge of etiquette, but they respect the old, love children, do as they please and act according to the dictates of their own consciences. So people do not pick up what others leave by the roadside, and there is no need to lock their doors at night. They love life, but they do not fear death. Their funeral service consists of joyful singing and dancing — the very opposite of the mournful and depressing funeral rites of the people of the Central Plain. The people in Jiande have found the secret of setting the mind free to wander in the void. They are united with each other, and they love each other, just as shoals of fish swim in the rivers and lakes. They never interfere with each other, nor clash with each other.

"My Lord, if you go there, your worries and troubles will disappear entirely."

"But Yue is far from here, and the road is very difficult. If I leave Lu, what vehicle will convey me thither?"

"When you cast off your haughty sovereign's manner, lead a life by your own labor and make friends with all, then you will naturally have your vehicle."

"I was born in the palace and have grown up in the palace. Wherever I am, I have people to keep my company and to serve me. Maids and eunuchs are always at my disposal. If I leave my palace to visit Yue, how can I leave them behind and travel alone? Besides, who will provide me with food?"

"My Lord, your burden is too heavy. No wonder you are always unhappy.

"Just think, when you throw away the heavy load of the State of Lu, and float on the rivers and seas in a light boat to view boundless nature, what a carefree life you will lead! When you look back to see the people on the shore seeing you off and leaving one after another, and think of the poor people who are endlessly enmeshed in the net of worldly affairs, a feeling of pride will come into your heart. As you get farther and farther away from the vulgar world day after day, you will become happier and happier. You will live like an immortal in Heaven and do as you wish, unrestrained and without worries."

As he spoke, the memories of his journey to

the south flooded back into Zhuang Zhou's mind and his face became radiant.

Duke Jing, however, was too much of this world to be attracted by his visitor's beautiful vision. The thought of setting sail alone in a small boat and entrusting himself to nature frightened him. Abruptly, he said:

"The State of Lu was the home of Confucius. As a result, it is a land of ceremony and the rites. As the ruler of Lu, I am the recipient of special respect. With all its cares, my throne is dearer to me than some vision of lonely rapture in the State of Yue."

With that, he took his leave.

Zhuang Zhou spent the next few days sightseeing in Lu. But all the places he visited had connotations of Confucius and his teachings, and so he found them displeasing. He then joined his diplomatic companions on the next stage of their journey, to the State of Zhao.

A Champion Invisible Swordsman

Handan, the capital city of the State of Zhao (covering the central part of today's Shanxi Province and the southwestern part of Hebei Province), was a major city on the Central Plain. In 353 BC, Pang Juan, the great general of the State of Wei, captured Handan. Intervention by the powerful State of Qi resulted in Handan being restored to Zhao, but for the next few years relations between Zhao and Wei were fractious. In the meantime, Zhao was plotting with the State of Han to jointly attack Wei and carve up its territory between them. In order to break the alliance between Zhao and Han, Wei wanted to improve its relations with Zhao, which was the true destination of the mission sent by Duke King Hui of Wei. The mission's visit to Lu was a mere smokescreen to divert Han's attention.

At this time, Zhao was ruled by Marquis Su (r. 349 — 326 BC). The marquis was consumed with ambition to expand the territory of Zhao, and embarked on a campaign of turning all his subjects into fighting men. The State of Lu, he reasoned, was becoming weaker and weaker because its ideology was the Confucian one of harmony, whereas the states of Wei, Qi and Qin were becoming stronger all the time because they elevated military might and the soldierly virtues.

This ambition became a mania with Marquis Su, so much so that he insisted that all his people learn swordsmanship. Official posts were allocated on the basis of the standard of a man's skill with the sword, and not on his learning or wisdom. The fields were neglected, as the farmers spent most of their time practicing swordsmanship. Traders neglected their business in their pursuit of the deadly art, and renowned swordsmen from every state flocked to the marquis' palace, where duels to the death took place.

This abnormal state of affairs, which threatened the very existence of Zhao, caused the marquis' son, the heir-apparent Kui, great anxiety. In private, he discussed with his close friends how they could persuade the marquis to see the error of his ways and return his state to one in which agriculture and trade flourished, and men of learning and statesmanlike qualities filled the administration. Kui even offered a huge reward for anyone who could get his father to shake off his obsession with swordsmanship; but there were no takers, as Marquis Su was notorious for his fiery temper and cruelty.

One day, one of his friends said:

"Sir, I have heard that there is a man called Zhuang Zhou in the mission from the State of Wei which has recently arrived in Handan. It is said that this man has an extraordinary gift of eloquence. He has traveled widely, had discussions with the ruler of Wei, and even denounced Confucius in the presence of the duke of Lu himself. His theories have a following of enlightened persons, forming a philosophical school. Perhaps this Zhuang Zhou can convince our sovereign to return to the path of reason."

Kui was delighted with this suggestion, and sent a servant with 1,000 pieces of gold to call on Zhuang Zhou at the state guesthouse.

Zhuang Zhou listened to the servant's explanation of the State of Zhao's woes. Then, without accepting the gold, he commented:

"Indeed, I have seen that the farmland of this state is neglected. And of course I could not help noticing people practicing with the sword everywhere. So I immediately sensed that all was not well here. Please ask your master to call on me to discuss how to solve this problem."

Kui, who had been forewarned of Zhuang

Zhou's unconventional ways, was not surprised to see his gift of gold still in the hands of his servant. But he asked:

"Sir, your granting me an audience raises hope in my breast that you are willing to help our state. Why, then, have you not accepted my gift?"

Zhuang Zhou replied:

"If I fail to convince your father to abandon his fixation with swordsmanship and return to a normal method of governance, he will have me executed. What use would this gold be to me then? If, however, I succeed, I will have done a great service to the State of Zhao. Such a service cannot be bought for all the gold in the world."

Kui recognized that Zhuang Zhou was a truly virtuous sage. But then a troubling thought occurred to him:

"My father, I'm afraid, will grant an audience to nobody but a swordsman."

Zhuang Zhou received this news with equanimity.

"Your Excellency," he said, "what your father sees are swordsmen with swords. I am a swordsman without a sword. I will use my unrivaled invisible sword to meet your father and his swordsmen with visible swords, and give them a crushing defeat."

"My invisible sword can defeat any visible

sword. I, an invisible swordsman, can defeat any visible swordsman. Because the invisible sword is a righteous sword, it is matchlessly sharp. An invisible swordsman is a wise person, and therefore all-conquering. Please make the arrangements for me to meet your father. I will surely turn the marquis away from the superficial flashing of visible swords and teach him to prefer the deeper penetration of the invisible sword."

Kui, however, insisted that the only way Zhuang Zhou would be able to enter the palace would be if he dressed like a swordsman and carried a sword. Zhuang Zhou reluctantly agreed, and accompanied the heir-apparent clad in this awkward garb.

It happened that a versatile swordsman from the State of Yan was that day showing off his unrivalled prowess by cutting to pieces all comers in the presence of Marquis Su. Zhuang Zhou watched this horrifying performance without blinking an eye. When the man from Yan had dispatched his last opponent, and was standing around looking for another, Zhuang Zhou whispered to Kui:

"Now is the time to introduce me to your father."

Kui, in great trepidation, introduced Zhuang Zhou to Marquis Su, who asked:

"What particular skill do you have with the sword."

Zhuang Zhou replied:

"I can walk a thousand *li* at a stretch, killing a man every ten steps."

The marquis turned to the man from Yan. "Tell Mr. Zhuang about your skill," he instructed.

The burly native of Yan said:

"My swordsmanship is spirited inwardly, but is easy outwardly. It looks like a beauty from the State of Chu, but moves like a tiger. Whoever acquires my skill will be equal to one thousand men. If you don't believe this, I will be pleased to give you a demonstration. But I warn you that you will not live to benefit from the enlightenment."

Marquis Su, thinking that Zhuang Zhou would be no match for the stalwart from Yan, frowned, and said to the visitor: "Is your sword capable of defending you in such a contest?"

Zhuang Zhou replied: "Your Highness, my sword is a treasure among swords. It can be longer or shorter, thick or thin. When I wield it, it can stand between Heaven and Earth. When I call it back, it can be hidden between two fingers."

He paused, while the others standing around were puzzled over his words. Then he continued:

"Let me explain that there are three types of sword in the world. They fall into three categories: One, the sword of the Son of Heaven; two, the swords of the princes and dukes; and three, the swords of the common people."

"What does the sword of the Son of Heaven look like?" asked Marquis Su, eagerly. The marquis had always been obsessed with the ambition to conquer all the rival states and make himself the Son of Heaven.

Zhuang Zhou replied:

"The sword of the Son of Heaven has the city of Xigu in the State of Yan and the Stone City beyond the Great Wall as its tip, Mt. Taishan in the State of Qi as its blade, the states of Jin and Wei as its back, the states of Zhao and Song as its guard and the states of Han and Wei as its handle. It is encircled by the Siyi Mountains, wrapped by the four seasons, surrounded by the Bohai Sea, bound by Mt. Hengshan, restricted by the five primary elements of metal, wood, water, fire and earth, judged by punishment and virtue, enlightened by Yin and Yang, held by spring and summer, and activated by autumn and winter.

"When such a sword is extended forward, there is nothing ahead. When it is lifted up, there is nothing above. When it is pressed down, there is nothing below. And when it is thrust aside, there is nothing by it. With this sword, you can slice the floating clouds above and sever the veins of the Earth below. Wherever it goes, it is invincible. Whoever obtains this sword can cow the princes and dukes, overawe the world and command everything. This is the sword of the Son of Heaven."

The marquis then asked:

"What does the sword of the princes and dukes look like?"

Zhuang Zhou was sure of his victory. He knew that the marquis, being a man consumed by ambition, was ensnared by his discourse. He continued:

"The sword of the princes and dukes has intelligent and brave men as its tip, clean and incorruptible men as its blade, able and virtuous men as its back, loyal and steadfast men as its edge, and men of outstanding abilities as its handle.

"When such a word is extended forward, there is nothing ahead. When it is lifted up, there is nothing above. When it is pressed down, there is nothing below. When it is thrust aside, there is nothing by it. Above, it circles Heaven and can follow the sun, the moon and the stars. Below, it squares the earth and can follow the four seasons. In the middle, it complies with the popular will and can pacify a region. This sword, when moved, shakes like thunder. No one within its reach will be disobedient. They must obey the orders of the sovereign. This is the sword of the princes and dukes."

This struck a chord in the heart of Marquis Su. After all, he was of the rank of the princes and the dukes, but had yet to take hold of the sword of the princes and dukes, as described by Zhuang Zhou. So he asked Zhuang Zhou to tell him about the third kind of sword, that of the common people.

Zhuang Zhou complied:

"As for the sword of the common people, most of its wielders have their hair disheveled and wear a bottle-like hat tied under the chin by a tasseled string. They wear short robes and strut around with staring eyes. They are taciturn, and delight in killing their rivals in public, and slice them up like offal. The sword of the common people has no more meaning than a cockfight.

"Once such a sword is used, a life is lost. This sword will bring a state nothing but mutual slaughter, ruined farmland and debilitated national strength. Your Highness aimed at picking up the sword of the Son of Heaven, but you've picked up the sword of the common people. What a pity!"

The marquis sat in abashed silence. The

swordsman from Yan broke the ice.

"Your Highness," he cried, "after hearing this gentleman's remarks, I find that I have come within a hair's breadth of harming the cause of you and your state. I beg you will allow me to depart."

Turning to Zhuang Zhou, he said:

"Thank you, sir, for enlightening me as to the baseness of my calling."

The swordsman from Yan kowtowed to the marquis, and left the hall, vanquished by the champion invisible swordsman. The heir-apparent of the Stae of Zhao couldn't help admiring Zhuang Zhou for his eloquence.

Marquis Su hosted a banquet for Zhuang Zhou that very evening. During the feasting, Zhuang Zhou noticed that the ruler of Zhao looked pensive, and seemed to have no appetite. After a while, he said:

"If Your Highness will permit me to say so, I think I know what is on your mind. But let me assure you that the sword of the Son of Heaven is within your grasp."

The marquis brightened visibly.

"It is?" he gasped. "Pray tell me how I can obtain it."

Zhuang Zhou replied:

"If you can fix your vital energy on tranquility,

keep your mind void and calm, govern the state by doing nothing, and follow the will of Heaven and the will of the people, you will be able to saunter within the bounds of the sword of the Son of Heaven and make it the instrument of your own rule."

The marquis thereupon eagerly accepted Zhuang Zhou's advice to dismiss the swordsmen, put men of learning and virtue in official posts, and return the common people to the diligent working of their fields. Both he and the heir-apparent Kui urged Zhuang Zhou to stay in Zhao as senior advisor to the court, but Zhuang Zhou refused with thanks. As soon as the diplomatic mission from Wei had finished its business, he departed with it for Daliang.

Returning Home

Soon after returning to Wei, Zhuang Zhou paid
a call on his old friend Prime Minister Hui Shi.
Hui Shi had already heard of Zhuang Zhou's
exploits in Lu and Zhao, and assured him that
his reputation had begun to spread far and wide.
Hui Shi, however, was unhappy. He confided to
Zhuang Zhou that he had been unable to dis-
suade the ruler of Wei from plotting an attack on
the State of Qi.

Indeed, Zhuang Zhou had noticed that the
capital was abustle with military preparations. He
urged Hui Shi to retire from public life and return
to live in seclusion on Mt. Mengshan, but the
prime minister felt that his duty was to continue
to work for peace no matter how remote that
goal seemed.

Zhuang Zhou thereupon requested an audience with King Hui. But when he found that all
his eloquence fell on deaf ears, as the ruler of
Wei was bent on war come what may, he washed
his hands of Wei and its fate, and set off back to

his home village.

It was winter, and Zhuang Zhou made slow progress as he trudged through the snow. But finally, on the eighth day of his journey, he saw the welcome bulge of Mt. Mengshan looming in the distance. He hurried forward, and as he did so, he tripped over a snow-covered hump by the roadside. Picking himself up, he saw that it was a young girl. A bowl and a stick, the hallmarks of a beggar, by her side told Zhuang Zhou a tragic tale, not uncommon in those days.

The girl was still breathing faintly, although she was obviously not far from death. Zhuang Zhou hoisted her onto his back and stumbled as best he could to his old home. There, he and his mother, Hui Ming, put the girl to bed, and when she showed signs of stirring, fed her a few spoonfuls of ginger soup.

The next day, the girl had made a full recovery. It turned out that her name was Yan Yu, and she was 19 years old. She had been born in a small village in the State of Wei, close to the frontier of Song. Her father had been conscripted for one of the ruler of Wei's endless wars years before, and had died on the battlefield. What little her mother and she could produce on their farm had been taken from them as tax, and the pair had had no choice but to take to the road as beggars. Her mother had perished in the same snowstorm which had nearly snatched her own life from her.

Yan Yu's tragic story struck a sympathetic chord in Hui Ming's heart, for she had had the same lot as the poor girl in her early days. That same day, Hui Ming adopted Yan Yu as her daughter.

When Zhuang Zhou arose the following morning, he found Yan Yu already helping his mother to prepare breakfast. She was dressed in a neat new set of clothes that Zhuang Zhou's mother had sat up half the night making for her.

Zhuang Zhou was eager to pay a call on his brother's family. As he stepped out of the doorway, he found himself in a silvery-white world. Mt. Mengshan raised its hoary head, looking like a dignified sage of old, Mengze Lake was a sparkling mirror, and the Menghe River curled like a sleeping dragon. His native place had never been so dear to him. Here was the grave of his father, and also the school where he received his early enlightenment; his mother now had a willing helper; his wise old friend the fisherman was close by, and also his beloved brother and sister-in-law — perhaps this was where he belonged, after all?

Settling Down to Family Life

Yan Yu quickly recovered her youthful vigor and luster. She was now a pretty girl in the flower of her youth. She flitted around the house and courtyard like a butterfly, bringing new life and zest to all around her. She had truly become an indispensable member of the family.

Since Yan Yu came, Zhuang Zhou felt that his life was much fuller, much maturer. Yan Yu was gentle by nature and fond of laughing. Zhuang Zhou found her tinkling laughter better than any music.

So, the life of the family was extremely harmonious and joyful.

Paying homage at his father's grave, Zhuang Zhou found recollections of his father flooding back. He felt that his love and respect for the people, the importance he attached to the people, the benefit he gave to the people and his readiness to devote his life to the people were perhaps all due to the influence of his father when he was a child. Even the help his father gave to his mother and the help he himself gave to Yan Yu were alike.

His next duty was to call on the old fisherman. But to his dismay, he found the thatched cottage empty and dilapidated. The horse too had disappeared. It was with a feeling of deep sadness that he went on to Hui Ze's home.

Hui Ze was now a married man with two sons. The two of them chatted about old times, during which time Zhuang Zhou started to appreciate the joys and advantages of married life .

The winter departed, and spring came. Zhuang Zhou and Yan Yu became busy with the farm work, while Zhuang Zhou's mother did the household chores. Zhuang Zhou's brother also helped with the farm work whenever he could tear himself away from his business activities.

Zhuang Zhou found working in the fields pleasant, especially with Yan Yu working beside him. He felt that human hands should, first of all, be used for labor, for growing crops, and then for writing, doing business, making crafts and practicing martial arts. But the Son of Heaven, the dukes and princes, and Confucius had reversed this order of priorities. In the course of the labour, he found that the earth was selfless and fair. If you sowed cereals, you got cereals, and if you sowed beans, you got beans. What dropped was your sweat, but what grew was life-giving grain. Labor was the treasure on which man depended for survival. The more labor you put in, the better the crop. From Yan Yu he learned how clever and great females were.

One day, while he and Yan Yu were taking a rest on the slope of Mt. Mengshan, the girl reached over to pick a golden flower. Stumbling on a rock, Yan Yu started to roll down the slope. Instantly, Zhuang Zhou rushed to save her. The two of them rolled down together until they stopped on a flat piece of ground with a carpet of green grass.

Zhuang Zhou held Yan Yu tightly in his arms, while Yan Yu closed her eyes. After a long while, Zhuang Zhou put one of his hands into her soft hair while using the other to wipe the sweat off her face gently. Only then did Yan Yu open her big and bright eyes. She looked at him, but still lay quietly in his arms. It was the first time that they had been so close to each other. At this moment, a pair of magpies started twittering. They were building a nest together as the foundation for their future. Zhuang Zhou and Yan Yu knew what was in each other's hearts, and hugged each other tightly.

Zhuang Zhou and Yan Yu sat on the grass

quietly for a long time. They found that they had sowed the seed of love between them in the course of their farm work in the past months and loved each other to such an extent that neither could leave the other.

Zhuang Zhou picked the golden flower which Yan Yu had failed to pick, and inserted it in her hair bun. To the sky, to the earth, to the sun, to the magpies and to Yan Yu, he said:

"The male energy is so strong and the female energy is so gentle and soft. When the two of them melt together, indescribable happiness results. Time will solidify, the world will be more lustrous, and the male and female energies will drift freely in space."

After he finished speaking, he and Yan Yu hugged each other tightly again.

In the evening, Zhuang Zhou told his mother of his feelings, and said that he wished to marry Yan Yu. To his surprise, his mother gave her unhesitating consent.

Zhuang Zhou's brother Zhuang Yan insisted that there should be a matchmaker hired, a lucky date chosen and a solemn wedding ceremony held. He also said that he would bear all the expenses of the marriage.

Zhuang Zhou did not agree. He said that there was a lucky date every day, and that there would be a full moon the following day as a sign of happiness. A matchmaker was not needed, either, he said, as it was the will of Heaven and Earth that he and Yan Yu should be united in matrimony. And Zhuang Zhou was glad that Mother saw eye to eye with him on this point.

Following the wedding, it seemed to Zhuang Zhou and Yan Yu that Mt. Mengshan was greener than ever, that Mengze Lake was clearer than ever, and that the Menghe River rushed along more jubilantly. Everything in the world looked beautiful. Zhuang Zhou's mother smiled all day long. Since she had no more worries, she looked younger and stronger.

One day, two officials from the Song court called at Zhuang Zhou's home. They brought costly gifts with them, and one said: "Sir, our sovereign has heard of the way you offered advice to the rulers of Wei, Lu and Zhao. He wishes to benefit from your wisdom by having you constantly by his side."

Hearing this, Zhuang Zhou smiled faintly and asked:

"Have you never seen an ox that is to be sacrificed? It is adorned so beautifully and fed so carefully. But some day it will be taken to the Ducal Temple and slaughtered on the altar. By that time, it will be impossible for the ox to be a lone bull in the wilderness. I'd rather be a lone bull than an ox slaughtered for sacrifice on an altar. Please tell the duke that I have no time to see him."

As he said this, he returned the gifts to the two men, and they had no choice but to leave.

Zhuang Zhou's mother had expected this reply, but Yan Yu was surprised. She asked:

"Do you really have such an aversion to becoming an official?"

"Yes," replied her husband. "I don't want to be a tool of the dukes and princes. If I had wanted to be an official, I would have become the tutor of a ruler long ago. But if I had done so, I would never have met you. In that case, my life would have been meaningless."

How the happy time flew! The spring of another year came round before they knew it, and Yan Yu gave birth to a boy. It had the good points of the looks of the father and the mother, a pair of big eyes, a broad brow and a tall figure. What a lovely baby he was!

The birth of the baby brought even more happiness to the household. But for Zhuang Zhou it also brought a new worry: How could he feed a family of four on their small plot of land? Moreover, Yan Yu was now too busy looking after the baby to help him with the farm work, and his mother was too old to do much around the house any longer. His feelings revolted against the idea of becoming an official; his ideas were too unorthodox for anyone to hire him as a teacher in a school; and he was already too old to learn a trade. Then he suddenly remembered how his father had earned a decent living as the supervisor of a market.

"Surely, as a minor official in charge of concrete affairs, I would not be doing any harm to the common people, would I?" he thought. "There is a government lacquer plantation on the northern side of Mt. Mengshan. Why should I not get a job there?"

When he told Yan Yu of his plan, she said:

"But I thought you were dead set against serving in an official post?"

"A person is constantly changing. Haven't you yourself changed from one person to two persons?"

His wife still had doubts.

"You sent the duke's men packing last year. I doubt if he will be ready to grant your request after that," she objected.

Zhuang Zhou, however, was confident:

"The dukes and princes of all the states are all eager to get me, as if I would be an ornament on

155

their hats, and especially our own Duke Ticheng. My good friend Hui Shi is now the Prime Minister of the State of Wei. I only have to write to him, asking him to put in a word for me with the prime minister of Song. Wei is a powerful state, and Song has to bow to its wishes."

So, Zhuang Zhou wrote a letter to Hui Shi. It was delivered by his brother Zhuang Yan, who had scheduled a business trip to Daliang. Sure enough, it was not long before Duke Ticheng sent a man to appoint Zhuang Zhou supervisor of the Mt. Mengshan Lacquer Plantation.

This plantation was the largest one run by the Song government. The lacquer trees were tall and straight, and stood neatly in rows like soldiers. At this time of year, under the trees were flowers in full bloom and a carpet of green grass, with bees buzzing and butterflies dancing. This filled Zhuang Zhou with delight. He disliked pompous palaces with their stuffy officials; he preferred the fields, and the mountain forests and wildernesses. Supervising the plantation was the perfect occupation, he thought. Here, he could get a salary to support his family, mingle with nature in all its simplicity, and keep himself far from the corrupting influence of political intrigue.

Some 20 years previously, he, Hui Shi and Hui Ze had once been chased out of the plantation while playing around there. That was the first and only time he had entered the place. Who would have thought that he would return in the role of supervisor? Truly, life was unpredictable!

On the first day in his new post, Zhuang Zhou toured the plantation. He watched the lacquer trees being tapped, and buckets of raw lacquer being carried to the processing plant to be refined into lacquer which gave furniture a beautiful sheen. The plantation was also home to government-run handicrafts workshops, such as a woodworking mill, a blacksmith's shop, a coppersmith's shop and a tannery.

Zhuang Zhou was deeply impressed by the skill of the artisans in turning crude raw materials into fine utensils and ornaments. It struck him that they were the most intelligent and cleverest people in the world, and he looked forward to sharing their lives.

When Zhuang Zhou went home and told his mother and wife about his impression of the lacquer plantation and how pleased he was with his appointment, they too were very happy. The family now settled into a life of joyous comfort, freed from all cares. The baby was now one month old, and called Zhuang Yuan.

But, in the words of Lao Zi, the founder of Taoism: "Good fortune lurks within bad; bad fortune lurks within good." Just as spring was changing into summer, Zhuang Zhou's mother fell ill, and died before a doctor could be summoned.

That evening, there was an unseasonable thunderstorm, which however scarcely drowned the mouring cries of the Zhuang family.

As he laid his mother to rest on Mt. Mengshan, Zhuang Zhou intoned an elegy, which read in part:

"My mother had a noble character and unimpaired integrity. She taught her children to eliminate the false and retain the true. She was sincere in her behavior toward people. Although she was poor all her life, she managed the household cleverly, and even helped the needy and relieved the distressed. She knew her children and her own heart as clearly as a glittering candle. She did her best to guide the future of my brother and me. She took every care of her daughters-in-law and grandchildren. When she died at 65, she looked like a rainbow. She'll remain in my heart for life, and my memory of her will grow with each passing day. May mother rest in peace and return to Heaven."

He then sprinkled wine over the grave.

Immediately after the funeral, Zhuang Zhou took Yan Yu and their son and moved their residence to the lacquer plantation.

Supervising the Mt. Mengshan Lacquer Plantation

His job at the lacquer plantation brought Zhuang Zhou into contact with new people, new experiences and new ideas. It was a totally different life from the one he had led previously — a far cry from his travels, farming and discourses with sovereigns.

It turned out that most of the workmen in the lacquer plantation were slaves who labored there from generation to generation; others were criminals banished to the plantation. The working conditions were harsh. The former plantation supervisor had been a sadistic tyrant who held human life cheap and had the workers flogged at the drop of a hat.

Zhuang Zhou wasted no time banning the use of whips and other instruments of punishment. He instructed his subordinates to treat the workers kindly, remembering that they were fellow human beings. At first, not only did his assistants find these orders strange; the workers too were puzzled, never having been treated as anything but beasts of burden before.

One day, Zhuang Zhou saw a snowy-haired old man bent almost double under the weight of the lacquer buckets he was carrying, one in each hand.

"How long have you been working here?" Zhuang Zhou asked.

The old man, who had never been addressed in such gentle tones before, was too startled at first to reply. Zhuang Zhou repeated his question, and finally the old man stammered:

"Sir, I've been working here all my life. I was born here, as my father too was a slave. My son was also born here, and started to work as soon as he was able to lift a bucket of lacquer."

"What's your name?" was Zhuang Zhou's next question, but because the workers were never addressed by their names on the plantation the old man had some difficulty remembering it. After some deep thought, he said:

"Sir, it's Bai Xin, which means 'condemned to work hard all my life in vain'."

It was then that Zhuang Zhou noticed, with a shock, that the old man's back was covered with scars, evidently left by innumerable applications of the lash. A sudden impulse made him grasp

Bai Xin's hand; it was as hard and callous as an oak tree. He said:

"Bai Xin, you have spent too many years at this dreadful toil. From tomorrow, you'll help me in the office, counting the buckets of lacquer."

The old man dropped on his knees, and kowtowed with a rapidity that belied his years, tears streaming from his eyes. The other laborers looked on in astonishment at this unprecedented scene of kindness reciprocated by gratitude.

On the following day, Bai Xin reported to the office, and began his new job of counting the buckets of lacquer. Being relieved of his previous back-breaking task, he soon found himself light-hearted and enthusiastic about his job. What was more, a few days later he was the recipient of another — and equally unexpected — act of kindness, when Yan Yu presented him with a newly made tunic, designed to display his new authority. Bai Xin again found his eyes misted over later when he learned of Yan Yu's identity.

But Zhuang Zhou's efforts to get his subordinates to treat the workers humanely did not proceed without obstacles.

One day, Bai Xin, who had become Zhuang Zhou's eyes and ears on the plantation, reported to his master that one of the guards was whipping a laborer. He reminded Zhuang Zhou that instances of a slave being whipped to death had not been uncommon under the previous supervisor. Zhuang Zhou hurried to the spot, and there he saw a burly guard lashing at a young workman who had already collapsed on the ground.

"What in Heaven's name is going here?" cried Zhuang Zhou. "You there! Hold that whip hand!"

The guard protested:

"Sir, this good-for-nothing was loafing on the job. They are all the same, Sir. They won't lift a finger if you don't beat them!"

Zhuang Zhou bent over and asked the worker:

"What's wrong?"

"My Lord, I am ill, and have diarrhea," the workman gasped. "Four times in a row I have had to stumble into the bushes."

"Don't listen to him, Sir! It's just an excuse!" cried the guard.

Zhuang Zhou said, calmly:

"Well, we'll soon find out, won't we? Let this man lead us to the evidence."

He ordered the guard to help the laborer to his feet, and to follow him into the bushes. Sure enough, four piles of evidence convinced Zhuang Zhou that the man had been telling the truth. The guard softened, like a pricked balloon.

"So," said Zhuang Zhou accusingly to the guard, "you knew very well that this man was ill, and you not only forced him to work, but whipped him because he could not keep up with the others! What have you to say for yourself?"

The other was speechless.

Zhuang Zhou turned to the worker. "Take the whip and give him a sound beating," he ordered.

"Sir, I dare not, for the life of me," said the victim, aghast.

Zhuang Zhou snatched the whip from the guard, but instead of beating him, he simply said:

"You are fired. Get out of my sight!"

By this time, a crowd of workers had gathered round to view this amazing scene, neglecting their work and forgetful of their old fears. It seemed to them as if their world had been turned upside down, as they watched one of the hated guards scuttling away, his tail between his legs, and, moreover, castigated by the supervisor himself for beating a slave!

From then on, the workers at the plantation threw themselves heart and soul into their tasks. There were no more whippings and no more slacking off. The production of lacquer increased, so that not only were the government's needs met, but the surplus could be sold to generate more income. This was a concrete example of the benefits of Zhuang Zhou's theory of "governing by doing nothing."

One fine autumn evening, Zhuang Zhou and Yan Yu were playing with their child, now nearly one year old, on the meadow outside the plantation, when a fine-looking young man approached, and suddenly kowtowed to Zhuang Zhou. The latter hastened to raise the stranger, but the youth refused to rise until he had completed three full obeisances. He then said:

"Sir, I have come specially to thank you for saving my life, and to ask you to accept me as one of your pupils."

Astonished, Zhuang Zhou asked the young man who he was, and what he meant by 'saving his life.'

"My name is Lin Qie," came the reply. "I am from the State of Wei. Some years ago at Daliang, you saved not only my life but that of my mother also, with a present of 50 taels of silver."

Zhuang Zhou laughed aloud with pleasure. So his generous gesture had not been in vain! He turned to the mystified Yan Yu, and explained the incident when he had insisted that he be arrested by the youth, who was then a teenager, and given over to Hui Shi. But, as for taking Lin Qie as a pupil, Zhuang Zhou sighed, and said:

"I made a decision long ago not to take pupils or disciples, not to give lectures or gather a following around me. That way, I would be simply following in the footsteps of Confucius, and bequeathing troubles to later generations. I dare not to be a master of others. I advise you, if you are a seeker of wisdom, to do what I did — travel extensively, learn more, see more, think deeply and fathom the ways of the world and Nature."

At this point, Yan Yu intervened:

"My dear," she pointed out, "have you not said many times that everything in the world is in a continuous state of change? Your thinking also changes. This is one situation and your past decision was taken in another. Why not accept this young man as your first pupil?"

Zhuang Zhou laughed again.

"Well, it seems that I, the teacher, have learned something even before I've accepted my first pupil! Very well, Lin Qie, from today we will learn from each other by exchanging views. We will not discuss the way to an official career or how rulers may best order their realms."

Lin Qie replied:

"I do not seek an official post, nor do I hanker after wealth. I just want to study your teachings and grasp the true meaning of life. I will endeavor to live up to your expectations."

His accidental meeting with Lin Qie caused Zhuang Zhou to think deeply about how everything in the world was accidental and held something that was too abstruse to grasp. As to the relations between him and Yan Yu and between him and Lin Qie, there was something unknown that tied them together. All things that were tied together like this constituted the world. And the world depended on space and time for its existence. The only eternal thing was the Tao. He then appreciated what Lao Zi meant when he said:

"A mixture of something existed before Heaven and Earth. It was silent and invisible. It is independent of other things and undergoes no change. It moves all the time, and never ceases. It can be regarded as the root source of all things in Heaven and on Earth. I don't know what its name is. Let's call it the 'Tao' (way) for the moment."

On their way home, Lin Qie told Zhuang Zhou what had happened after their parting in Daliang. After receiving the 50 taels of silver, he and his mother had opened a small grocery. The boy then devoted himself to studying. He read the works of all the leading philosophers — Confucius, Mo Zi and many others. But Zhuang Zhou's ideas were the ones that held the key to the secrets of life and the universe, he was convinced. Only the fact that he was his mother's sole support prevented him from leaving Daliang and going in search of the man of supreme wisdom. Only when his mother had passed away did he finally shake the dust of Daliang from his feet and wander in search of Zhuang Zhou.

Zhuang Zhou had acquired a new assistant in his work. While the two of them looked after the plantation they held constant discussions on philosophical matters. Lin Qie often raised new and absorbing questions, which made Zhuang Zhou think deeply and promoted the development and maturity of his thinking.

Aspiration Achieved

In 328 BC, Duke Ticheng was ousted from power in the State of Song by his younger brother Yan, and fled to the State of Qi.

Yan soon proved himself a tyrant. His agents scoured the realm for beautiful women to stock his harem. He squeezed the common people for every last coin and every last ear of corn in taxes to fund an extravagent program of building palaces and pleasure grounds. In preparation for an insane scheme to challenge the mighty states of Qi, Wei and Chu, military preparations were stepped up to fever pitch. Not the least of his alarming eccentricities was his habit of hanging up a leather bag filled with blood, and shooting it with an arrow, so that the blood spurted on the onlookers. The bag represented the Emperor of Heaven, whom Yan boasted that he would shoot down from the sky.

One day, while taking a stroll on Mt. Mengshan, lost in contemplation, Zhuang Zhou noticed a cicada enjoying the cool shade under a tree leaf and chirping melodiously. However, it was unaware of a mantis perched on a nearby twig, ready to pounce on it. The mantis, in turn, was oblivious to a bird perched higher on the tree and intent on making the mantis its prey. All three, absorbed in their personal ambitions, were ignorant of the approach of Zhuang Zhou himself, who could, if he had so wished, become another predator in the chain.

This made Zhuang Zhou think:

"Is not all life like this? We are so wrapped up in our petty affairs that we fail to notice the nemesis which is approaching with soft footfalls."

He was rudely awakened to the truth of this insight later that day, when Lin Qie handed him a decree from Duke Yan ordering him to double the output of the lacquer plantation, on pain of death. Zhuang Zhou gave the decree a quick glance, and threw it onto the floor, with a guffaw. He then related to the astonished Lin Qie what he had seen that morning.

"Just like the cicada, the mantis and the bird, I too have somebody waiting to gobble me up!" he cried. "I'm now forty-one years old. Official life, even in this humble occupation, is not for me. Now is the time for me to retire to a life of meditation and study. If you wish to continue as my pupil, Lin Qie, you may accompany me."

The other readily agreed, and so Zhuang Zhou and his family and Lin Qie and his wife, Zi Ling, moved out of the lacquer plantation and back to Mengzhuang Village.

Zhuang Zhou's elder brother, Zhuang Yan, approved of Zhuang Zhou's decision to sever his ties with the government at this dangerous time when the throne of Song was occupied by a madman. Zhuang Yan had become a wealthy man through his business activities, and hastened to build a house for his younger brother, whom he was anxious to have living near him. For this task, among others, he engaged Zi Qing, Lin Qie's father-in-law, who was an outstanding carpenter.

As the house was being built, together with another one for Lin Qie, Zhuang Zhou could not help feeling the utmost respect for and wonder at the skill of Zi Qing. The master carpenter used no ruler or other tools, but measured with his eyes. Never was his judgment faulty. Zhuang Zhou also admired the skill of the masons, and that of the wives of himself and Lin Qie as they turned lumps of unappetizing-looking dough into delicious meals.

He looked at his own hands. They were worthless, he felt. Oh, he could speak volubly before sovereigns, and berate the most powerful figures in the land for incompetence and villainy, but what use was he now that he had retired? The common people did everything for him, while all he could do was to stand aside so as not to interfere with their work.

He recalled Zi Qing's greatest triumph.

A few years previously, the ruler of Song had ordered a wooden frame made for a set of chimes. Such a frame, from which hung a row of chimes of different sizes and pitches, required a high degree of craftsmanship. The frame would have animal figures carved on it to match the chimes, so that each chime would reproduce the cry of its animal.

Four craftsmen had already been put to death for producing unsatisfactory frames already, when Zi Qing was ordered to undertake the task. The frame was to be completed within 15 days. Inexplicably, Zi Qing did nothing for the first ten days but stroll in the mountains. For the last five days, he locked himself in his workshop, which was located near the lacquer plantation, allowing no one to disturb him, not even his apprentices.

On the day the frame was to be collected by the duke's officials, Zhuang Zhou, together with a crowd of others, hurried to Zi Qing's workshop. They were stunned by the masterpiece which appeared before their eyes:

On the brightly painted frame were carved birds and animals looking as true to life as if they had just been caught. The palace official who had been sent to inspect the work ordered a team of musicians to test the chimes. When they did so, the bigger chimes roared like lions and tigers, while the smaller ones gave out sounds as cheerful as the lark's song at daybreak and as clear as gold beads dropping on to a jade plate, and lingered as long as a fine drizzle. Zhuang Zhou closed his eyes, and the heavenly music wafted him to the realm of the Tao. This was an early instance of the influence of superb craftsmanship on Zhuang Zhou's philosophy of life.

Freed from the cares of his duties at the lacquer plantation, Zhuang Zhou indulged in a life of leisure, contemplation and profound discussion with Lin Qie. Their two families reclaimed land and enjoyed a bumper harvest that autumn. But Zhuang Zhou was too famous to escape the solicitations of the powerful for long, and one day a messenger from the State of Qi arrived with an invitation from Chunyu Kun, together with travelling expenses to Linzi (present-day Zibo, in Shandong Province), the capital of Qi.

Zhuang Zhou was both surprised and overjoyed. He had admired Chunyu Kun ever since his first, and so far only, meeting with him in Daliang some ten years previously. Chunyu Kun was erudite, and had a good moral character. He was good at citing parables to clarify problems and situations. Besides, with the harvest gathered in, there was little work left on the farm for the rest of the year. This was a golden opportunity, Zhuang Zhou felt. Besides, he could take Lin Qie with him to broaden the young man's horizons.

The evening before they left, Zi Qing brought a gift for Zhuang Zhou. It was a wooden figure of a dragon, but it was so magnificently carved that when Zhuang Zhou took it, he did so tenderly as if afraid that it would take wing and soar into the sky, so lifelike it was.

Zi Qing said:

"Sir, I have greatly benefited from your teachings. I spent three years completing this dragon, into which I poured my utmost energy and craftsmanship. I give it to you because only you, who knows the lofty nature of the dragon, can receive its spiritual influence."

He went on:

"There are many legends about dragons, and many fanciful descriptions of them, but no one has ever seen one. I first imagined it calmly, then thought of it carefully, painted it silently and carved it as I wished, so that my Heaven could conform to the material Heaven, and the material Heaven and my Heaven are combined into one in the natural world in the form of this dragon."

Linzi was a prosperous city at that time. Iron smelting, copper refining and textile industries flourished, and it boasted stores, workshops and fairs in abundance. It was a well-planned and sturdily built city of more than 30 sq km. The casual and cheerful attitudes of the local people, and the way they would break into extempore singing and dancing reminded Zhuang Zhou of the time he had spent in the states of Chu and Yue.

One of the first things Zhuang Zhou and Lin Qie did in Linzi was to accompany Chunyu Kun to pay their respects at the tomb of Yan Ying. The tomb was located near the center of the city, by the philosopher's former residence. Chunyu Kun explained:

"Yan Zi liked to listen to the voices of the common people, so he lived in the downtown district. He insisted that after his death his body be left in the downtown district. So his tomb was built here."

Zhuang Zhou commented:

"Yan Zi said: 'A man can be humble but not

lose his honor, and suffer injustice but remain upright, because he takes the people as the foundation.' I respect this true man of talent and virtue. If it had not been for him, Confucian doctrines would run rampant here, for he warned that the people would become poorer with each passing day if everything were done according to Confucius' doctrines. It was he who advised Duke Jing of Qi to drive Confucius out of the territory."

Turning to Lin Qie, he said:

"Let's salute this great philosopher who proposed that 'administration must conform to the people, and conduct must conform to the will of the gods.'"

All three of them then made deep bows to Yan Ying's tomb.

On the following day, Chunyu Kun took his guests in his carriage to the nearby Zishui River. They alighted at a bend of the river, where a large area of low-lying land was inundated to form a small lake. Lining the margins were poplars, willows and reed marshes. It was late autumn, and a gentle breeze created ripples across the water. Under the ripples was a complex world: water weeds covered the whole surface of the lake, and among the water weeds were carp, catfish, soft-shelled turtles, ricefield eels, snakeheaded fish, loaches, crabs, shrimps, and so on.

Chunyu Kun said:

"It is said that Yu the Great came here after taming the floods, and regulating the rivers and other waterways. He took a boat upstream to the source of this river. There he saw innumerable springs gushing out black waves. Hence the name 'Zishui,' the character zi meaning black. In fact, the water in the river is so clear that you can see to the bottom, which is covered with pure white sand. A kind of eel dwells in this river, which has no fins or scales. On each side of its head there is an orange-red ear. It is dark green, and shorter but bigger than the yellow eel. It can be as heavy as two and a half kg. The whole body has only one backbone, and no small bones. Its meat is white, tender and delicious. The entrancing taste will linger in your mouth for three days. If you cook one in a pot, everyone else will know, because the grease from the eel's body will stick to the pot."

Chunyu Kun, knowing that Zhuang Zhou was a keen angler, had sent men ahead to prepare rods and lines, and comfortable stools, ready for a day's fishing. Inviting Zhuang Zhou and Lin Qie to be seated, he said:

"I think the great Jiang Shang fished at this very spot 700 years ago."

"Then I'm sure to catch a Zishui eel by taking advantage of the Great Master Jiang Shang's spiritual influence," Zhuang Zhou said, only half in jest.

For several hours, they sat in the golden autumn sunshine in silence, gazing at the river. Chunyu Kun was the first to be lucky; he caught a red carp. Lin Qie eventually hauled in several fish of different types. But the float on Zhuang Zhou's fishing rod hardly even bobbed, until, just as the party was ready to leave the spot and return to the city, the float plunged deep into the water, and Zhuang Zhou felt a mighty force tugging at his rod. After a tremendous struggle, which attracted the attention of the others, he managed to land a Zishui River eel. The creature was found to weigh a record 3.5 kg!

King Xuan of Qi learned of the visit of the famous Zhuang Zhou only on the day of the latter's departure. He sent a swift messenger with a personal message to ask him to return. The man caught up with Chunyu Kun's carriage, which was taking Zhuang Zhou and Lin Qie back to Song, on the road. Reading the letter, Zhuang Zhou told Lin Qie:

"King Xuan is really fond of talented people. He wants me to teach at the Jixia Academy in

Linzi for a fat salary. How could he know, however, that Zhuang Zhou is a little bird unwilling to be shut in a cage for people to admire!"

He turned to the messenger, and said:

"I thank His Majesty for his kindness, but tell him that there is no place for Zhuang Zhou in the corridors or halls of power."

With that, he ordered his driver to continue westward.

Expressing Ideas Through Fables

Back in the bosom of his family, Zhuang Zhou hit on the idea of using fables to get his ideas across, ideas which many found puzzling when explained in the traditional scientific terms. He and Lin Qie drew on local sources, and these fascinating stories have been passed down from generation to generation for over 2,000 years, and will be passed down forever.

One day, a man called Sun Xiu came to call. He said to Zhuang Zhou:

"Sir, you are well known for advocating doing nothing. Now, I have not recommended myself for any official post, nor have I extended a helping hand to any person in distress. Is this in conformity with your doctrine of doing nothing? I fear I must have offended Heaven in some way, as my farm never yields a good harvest, and no sovereign seeks my advice."

Zhuang Zhou replied:

"Your way of doing nothing is not the true way of doing nothing. Today, I want to teach you how to be a virtuous man. A virtuous man forgets the vital organs of his body, forgets his ears, eyes, nose and mouth. He is in a constant state of trance, and travels beyond the dust and dirt. He enjoys leisure in the course of doing nothing. This is precisely the way to avoid all arrogance and grow great without seeking an official post.

"What you do is mere outward show. Expecting to become great in that way is like trying to catch the sun and the moon with your hands. It is impossible. A man like you is lucky if he can preserve his body from dumbness, blindness and lameness. Why should you blame Heaven?"

Sun Xiu left disheartened. Zhuang Zhou looked at the sky and breathed a long sigh.

When Lin Qie asked him why he sighed, Zhuang explained with a parable, as follows:

"Once upon a time, a beautiful bird came to the outskirts of the capital city of the State of Lu. It happened to be seen by the ruler of Lu. He liked it very much, and ordered his men to catch it and take it to the palace. There, he fed it the sumptuous dishes normally reserved for a chief minister and had court music played to entertain it. But the beautiful bird pined away, and died. If the bird had been allowed to dwell in the forests, float on the rivers and lakes, and eat insects and snakes it would have continued to thrive.

"Therefore, in doing anything, one should suit the medicine to the illness and offer advice suitable to the person who requests it."

One day, the local river supervisor Shang Li came to see Zhuang Zhou.

He and Zhuang Zhou had been on close terms while the latter was the lacquer plantation supervisor, but when Zhuang Zhou left the job and was no longer in favor at court, Shang Li had broken off their friendship. When Zhuang Zhou approached him to borrow some grain, Shang Li said:

"I cannot afford to lend you grain right now, but next year I will be able to lend you however much you wish."

This occasioned Zhuang Zhou to relate one of his famous parables to Shang Li:

"One day, when I was walking along a road, I suddenly heard someone calling me. I looked around, but saw nobody. When I looked down, it turned out to be a carp calling me from a dried rut. I went over to it, and asked, 'Is there anything I can do for you?' The carp, gasping, replied, 'I am a minister of the God of the East Sea. I was swept here by a rainstorm, and now I cannot get back. I will soon die, unless you bring a pail of water and put me in it.' I said, 'Of course, I can do that. But you must wait until I persuade the sovereigns of the states of Wu and Yue to allow me to use water from the Xijiang River.' Hearing this, the carp said, 'Distant water cannot quench present thirst. You'll find me in the dried fish market tomorrow'!"

With that, Zhuang Zhou left in a huff. He and Shang Li had never seen each other ever since.

On this occasion, Shang Li had come to gloat over how Zhuang Zhou had come down in the world.

"I really cannot understand," he said, "how a man supposedly as talented as you are, should prefer to hide himself away on a humble farm, when he can have riches and glory for the asking."

Zhuang Zhou thereupon told him another parable:

"A man called Wu Duan raised pigs specially for the palace sacrificial rites. One day, a piglet started scurrying around and squealing in the pigpen, as if it had a foreboding of its impending demise. Wu Duan tried to calm it by saying, 'Piglet, why should you be afraid of death? It is precisely because you are being reared for a sacrifice that you will have the best feed for a whole three months before you go to the magnificent altar of our ruler. Would you rather stay in this filthy sty for the rest of your life, eating coarse chaff?'

"The piglet was unconvinced. However, the very next day the court issued an order that Wu Duan was to move into the royal palace, and eat and sleep like the sovereign every day, and have official carriages and garments and beauties at his disposal. But after the sovereign died, he would be buried alive in the ruler's tomb as a sacrificial object. Wu Duan agreed happily, so as to convince the piglet to accept its fate."

Shang Li left, shaking his head in bewilderment.

Another butt of one of Zhuang Zhou's fables was the villainous Su Yu. He had used his cunning to escape from his predicament in the State of Wei, and wormed his way into the good graces of the tyrant Yan of Song. He too one day decided to call on Zhuang Zhou and sneer at this righteous man whom he had tried but failed to bring to ruin.

Dismounting from a sumptuous carriage, with the help of the duke's own attendants, Su Yu greeted Zhuang Zhou affably enough. Then he proceeded to contrast his own prosperity as a man of the world to the present low circumstances of Zhuang Zhou, who despised the world.

Thereupon, a new fable emerged. Lin Qie recorded it just as it fell from Zhuang Zhou's lips:

"Once upon a time there was a family which lived by a riverside. They eked out a meager living by weaving reed mats. One day, the son of this family, while swimming in the river, found a precious pearl. He took it home and handed it to his father, saying, 'We no longer have to weave reed mats, Father, now that we are wealthy.'

"However, his father, who had experienced the hardships of life, said to the boy: 'Alas, this is not good fortune but a disaster that has come upon us!' When his son asked him what he meant, the old man explained, ' This pearl belongs to the Black Dragon. You must have come upon it while the dragon was sleeping. When it wakes up, it will surely come looking for it. Far better to throw the pearl back into the river or crush it to powder!'"

Finding Su Yu staring blankly at him, Zhuang Zhou said:

"Our ruler Duke Yan is far more cruel than the Black Dragon. You surely obtained your fine clothes, carriage and entourage when the sovereign was asleep or distracted by his pleasures. When he returns to his senses, disaster will befall you."

Su Yu broke out in a cold sweat. He fell ill, and was confined to bed in Mengzhuang Village.

In the meantime, a new clique of courtiers had

gained the ascendancy at Duke Yan's court. They had murdered or expelled their rival group, which had included Su Yu. Fortunately for the latter, he had been overlooked in the general mayhem, as he had been absent from the court for months.

Su Yu learned his lesson. He turned over a new leaf, and joined Zhuang Zhou in the study and discussion of the Tao.

Finding Fulfilment Weaving Shoes

Because of his determination not to become soiled by accepting any of the invitations from powerful rulers, Zhuang Zhou became poorer and poorer. The main source of his and Lin Qie's livelihood was selling the fish they caught in Mengze Lake. However, this afforded them only a meager and unstable income.

But an unexpected disaster turned out to be a blessing, and revived their fortunes somewhat.

One day, after several hours of fishing and not catching even one fish, Zhuang Zhou and Lin Qie were forced to seek shelter from a fierce storm. Peering out into the pouring rain from the doorway of the tumbledown hut they had taken refuge in, Zhuang Zhou said:

"We can barely keep body and soul together simply by fishing. We must think of some way to supplement our income. But what else can we do?"

Lin Qie suddenly had an idea. Pointing to the vast expanse of reeds by the shores of the lake, he said:

"Why don't we weave shoes using the reeds as the raw materials? There is always a market for sturdy shoes, and, as you know, reeds are tough."

Zhuang Zhou acknowledged that he was right, and the two of them set to work right away cutting a bundle of reeds each. When they showed the reeds to Yan Yu and Zi Lin, the women could scarcely hold back their tears of joy, for now they would be able to help their husbands earn a good living.

Zi Lin had inherited some of her father's skill as a craftsman, while Yan Yu had learned the shoe-weaving skill from her mother-in-law Hui Ming and soon the two picked up the technique of making shoes that were hard-wearing and at the same time stylish. Zhuang Yuan, who was now a young man, also learned the craft quickly. Lin Qie's job was to gather the reeds, while Zhuang Zhou took the finished shoes to the market to sell them. Business was brisk, so that before long the two families left poverty behind, and finally had plenty to eat every day.

As he became more skilled as a salesman, Zhuang Zhou, now in his fifties, started to seek customers farther afield. He was soon a familiar sight in the markets of Mengyi, Suiyang and Taoyi, a commercial center in the northwest of today's

Dingtao County, Shandong Province. The news that the great philosopher was visiting their town drew crowds of people who wished to hear his words of wisdom, or just to gawk at him; either way, he ended up selling lots of shoes.

Zhuang Zhou found that this life suited him. The myriad little events which he observed on his travels and especially in the market places gave him great insights into human nature and much food for speculation.

Duke Yan, although an unlettered oaf, was proud of the fact that his state was home to a thinker of universal fame, and had often basked in the flattery of envoys from other states, who pretended to respect him as a patron of learning. But when he heard that Zhuang Zhou had been reduced to peddling shoes, he was horrified at the prospect of the derision of his fellow sovereigns. He thereupon sent a messenger to Zhuang Zhou's home with a present of a cartload of millet and a written invitation to him to choose any job he liked in the government.

To the messenger's surprise, Zhuang Zhou acted as though the offer was a personal insult, and sent him packing, together with the millet, which would have fed his family for a year.

The shoe business thrived so much that Zhuang

Zhou could afford to farm their products out to a man to sell the shoes for him. This left him free to help Lin Qie, lightening the latter's work and giving them both time to fish in Mengze Lake and engage in philosophical discussions in the evening.

Zhuang Zhou's reputation finally spread to the faraway State of Chu. The ruler of Chu, King Qingxiang, learned that the sage had once visited his state and often praised the way of life there. He sent two emissaries to invite Zhuang Zhou to become his prime minister.

The emissaries finally found Zhuang Zhou in Taoyi, fishing in the Pushui River. When they told him their errand, Zhuang Zhou replied with one of his parables:

"I've heard that there was once a divine turtle in the State of Chu. The ruler of Chu had it killed, and used its shell for divination. It was effective every time he divined. The other bones of the dead turtle were wrapped in a piece of rare silk cloth and kept in a beautiful bamboo box which now stands in a place of honor on the altar of the royal ancestral temple. Is this true?"

"Yes, it is," the envoys replied.

"What do you think: Would the turtle prefer to be dead and in a place of honor, with its shell revered by the sovereign, or would it prefer to be still dragging its tail in the mud?"

"Of course, the latter, Sir," said the visitors.

"In that case, gentlemen," said Zhuang Zhou, "I bid you farewell, as I prefer to drag my tail in the mud too!"

In the beautiful season of autumn, Hui Shi returned to his home village after 30 years' absence. Zhuang Zhou was surprised to see how old his friend had grown. Hui Shi's hair and beard were snowy white. He was somewhat humpbacked and walked haltingly. He was some years younger than Zhuang Zhou, but he looked older.

Zhuang Zhou immediately sent for their old classmate Hui Ze, and, together with Lin Qie, they all sat down to a simple feast.

It transpired that Hui Shi had fallen out of favor with King Xiang of Wei, who had fallen into a trap set by the chief minister Zhang Yi of the State of Qin to sow discord between him and Hui Shi and who had thus dismissed the latter from his post as prime minister. Hui Shi had travelled all the way to the State of Chu, where he offered to serve its sovereign. But King Huai of Chu was unwilling to offend the state of Qin, where Hui Shi was mistrusted or hated. Returning to his home state of Song, Hui Shi was received by Duke Yan. But Hui Shi's advocacy of benevolent rule clashed with the latter's wild ambition for military conquest, and so he once more left a court unemployed.

Soon after, King Xiang of Wei rehabitated Hui Shi, but the latter had not taken up his old post long before he was dismissed again by the capricious and fatuous sovereign. Totally disappointed, Hui Shi decided to settle down in Mengzhuang Village. When Zhuang Zhou went to congratulate him on building a house for himself, Hui Shi said:

"I had a dream last night, in which King Xiang asked me to take up my old post again. But I told him: 'I would rather be a weed growing on Mt. Mengshan than a pillar of the State of Wei. I would rather fish by Mengze Lake than be the prime minister in Daliang. Zhuang Zhou is far superior to me in talent and learning; yet he lives by selling shoes. I'm determined to follow his example. It's a pity that I lost my way for such a long time.' When I awoke, I knew what I must do — adopt your lifestyle."

"You should have woken up from your dreams a long time ago," said Zhuang Zhou.

Hui Shi prepared some food and wine, and the two friends were just settling down for a cosy chat when Zhuang Zhou's son, Zhuang Yuan, ran into the house, gasping for breath, and said:

"Father, come home quickly! Mother has fainted!"

Zhuang Zhou hurried home. Yan Yu lay on the couch, under the care of Lin Qie and his wife. Decades before, Zhuang Zhou remembered, his mother had been lying calmly like this before she died. He squatted down, taking one of Yan Yu's cold hands in one of his own, and smoothing her grey hair with the other. Yan Yu's once-bright eyes seemed to have become smaller and to have less luster.

Zhuang Zhou, whose researches into nature and the meaning of life had acquainted him with herbs and the preparation of medicine personally took charge of curing his wife's illness. With decoctions he had devised himself, he slowly nursed Yan Yu back to health. Before another spring came round, she was up and about, and had started making shoes again.

Into the Sunset

Pacing around his courtyard one bright spring morning, Zhuang Zhou suddenly felt intimations of mortality.

"I should put my thoughts into writing in the few years I have left," he thought to himself. "Confucius and Mo Zi went about peddling their ideas and gathered disciples by giving public lectures. Gui Gu Zi called persons of outstanding ability in the world together and taught them the strategy and skill of dealing with friends and enemies. The Jixia Academy, with large numbers of scholars, allowed different schools of thought to contend and each to express its views so as to spread them to the whole country. Jiang Shang and Sun Wu produced amazing works to be passed down forever. It's high time I did the same."

He then mused, "Lin Qie has written down many of my fables and stories, but it has not been done systematically, and cannot express clearly my knowledge of the world, my castigation of evils, my understanding of the Way of Heaven or my judgment of the different schools of thought."

He left the courtyard and wended his way toward Mt. Mengshan. His eyes swept over the enchanting scene — Mengze Lake as clear as a mirror, the sparkling Menghe River, the roadside flowers newly blossoming, and the vast blue sky. His mind made up, he retraced his steps homeward, where he lost no time getting to work writing his masterpiece of wisdom. He was then well into his sixties.

Zhuang Zhou's book consisted mainly of parables. The first chapter, "The Happy Excursion," starts as follows: "In the Northern Ocean there is a fish, by the name of Kun, which is many thousand *li* in size. This fish metamorphoses into a bird by the name of Peng, whose back is many thousand *li* in breadth. When this bird rouses itself and flies, its wings obscure the sky like clouds. When this bird moves itself in the sea, it is preparing to start for the Southern Ocean, the Celestial Lake."

The next chapter was called "On the Equality of Things." Zhuang Zhou read it aloud to Yan Yu:

"Nanguo Ziqi sat leaning on a table. He was looking heavenward and breathing gently. He seemed to be in a trance and unconscious of his body. Yancheng Ziyou, who was in attendance on him, asked, 'What is this? Can the body become thus like dry wood, and the mind like dead ashes? The man leaning on the table today is not he who was here before.'

"Nanguo Ziqi said, 'Yan, your question is very good. Just now, I lost myself, do you understand? You may have heard the music of man, but not the music of the Earth; you may have heard the music of the Earth, but not the music of Heaven.'

"Yancheng Ziyou said, 'I would like to ask for an explanation of these.'

"Nanguo Ziqi said: 'The breath of the universe is called the wind. At times it is inactive. When it is active, angry sounds come from every aperture. Have you not heard the growing roar? The imposing appearance of mountain forests, the apertures and cavities in huge trees many a span in girth: these are like nostrils, like mouths, like ears, like beam sockets, like goblets, like mortars, like pools, like puddles. The wind goes rushing into them, making the sounds of rushing water, of whizzing arrows, of scolding, of breathing, of shouting, of crying, of deep wailing, of moaning agony. Some sounds are shrill, some deep. Gentle winds produce minor harmonies; violent winds, major ones. When the fierce gusts pass away, all the apertures are empty and still. Have you not seen the bending and quivering of the branches and leaves?'"

Yan Yu said calmly: "The winds you write about are too mysterious for me. Why can't I distinguish them?"

"It is because you've concentrated your mind on the home," said her husband, "weaving shoes and taking care of the child. You've just listened with your ears and looked with your eyes; you have not concentrated your mind."

Shortly afterwards, as a pair of swallows were building a nest again under the eaves of Zhuang Zhou's house, Zhuang Yuan married a girl from a neighboring village.

That day, Yan Yu was blissfully happy. Although she was busy for the whole day, she was still in high spirits when the moon rose over Mt. Mengshan, as she now had someone to help her with the household chores. That night, she rested her head on Zhuang Zhou's arm, and said:

"If you had not saved me on that snowy day long ago, I would never have lived to savor the happiness that is my lot today."

Zhuang Zhou replied:

"You are my pillar. Without you, I could have accomplished nothing."

Rising early the following morning, and being careful not to wake Yan Yu, Zhuang Zhou went for a stroll on Mt. Mengshan. As he was returning, his son came rushing wild-eyed out of the gate.

"Father, come quick!" he shouted. "It's mother…"

A pang of fear stabbed at Zhuang Zhou's heart, spurring him to hurry inside. But he was too late: Yan Yu had departed this life.

Yan Yu had been the spark of Zhuang Zhou's being and the sole reason of his existence. Alas, she was now gone! How could he not help but be overwhelmed with grief!

The news of Zhuang Zhou's bereavement soon spread throughout the village, and all the neighbors and friends of the family came to express their condolences. Yan Yu was placed in a coffin, which was then put into a makeshift mourning shed, where Zhuang Zhou kept vigil.

When Hui Shi called, to his astonishment he found that Zhuang Zhou, far from being immersed in grief, was sitting on the ground and singing, all the while keeping time by beating on an upturned earthenware basin:

The snowflakes are swirling,
The north wind is howling.
There are one thousand roads,
But none can be chosen.

Heaven is supernatural,

It shows me the way.
I met Yan Yu by chance,
When she was suffering from cold and hunger in the
    wilderness.

In spring, the mountain flowers bloom,
Beautiful and charming.
Falling under the precipice,
The magpie sang with joy.

Let Nature take its course,
Be a happy couple for life.
Take pleasure in hardships,
Have noble character and heroic spirit.

She devoted herself to making shoes,
With a sharp mind and nimble hands.
Year in and year out,
Till the moon hangs on the tree.

My good wife,
My honor.
The wind assists me,
Let her be carefree.

She passed away so suddenly,
Feelings well up in my mind.
My pillar is gone,

Leaving me swaying in the snowstorm.

My wife has turned into clouds,
Gone with the wind.
Standing aloof and returning to the true,
What is there to worry about?

The wind scatters the clouds,
It is especially enchanting.
I am happy that my wife,
Is freed from troublesome toil.

I sing and I recite,
Let me bow.
We shall meet,
In the highest heavens.

When the chanting stopped, Hui Shi knelt before the bier, lit incense and bowed. Then he turned to Zhuang Zhou.

"My old friend," he said, with compassion, "I fear that this loss has unhinged your mind. Instead of mourning for your deceased wife, your unfailing helpmate through thick and thin, I find you here beating on a basin and singing. Are you not afraid that others will censure you for your lack of decorum?"

Zhuang Zhou explained:

"When she had just died, I could not help being affected. Soon, however, I examined the matter from the very beginning. At the very beginning, she was not living, having no form, nor even substance. But somehow or other there was then her substance, then her form, and then her life. Now, by a further change she has died. The whole process is like the sequence of the four seasons. While she is thus lying in the great mansion of the universe, for me to go about weeping and wailing would be to proclaim myself ignorant of the natural laws. In addition, I have further understood why the people of the State of Yue sing and dance at funeral services!"

After burying his wife, Zhuang Zhou became reticent. Although the son and daughter-in-law gave him every care, he found that without Yan Yu in his life, he was incomplete. He lived a secluded life. Mt. Mengshan and Mengze Lake seemed to become farther and farther from him.

After a period of pains, keeping aloof, loneliness and silence, he felt that he must speed up the progress and do his best to write as many articles as possible. Yan Yu's sudden death awakened him. He was, after all, an old man like the setting sun and the candle guttering in the wind. There were not many days left for him.

All in all, Zhuang Zhou was Zhuang Zhou.

With the help of Lin Qie and Zhuang Yuan, he did not do it at one go, but instead, wrote it slowly about health preservation. He did it out of his personal feeling about the flying dragon, the masterpiece of Zi Qing, which had been together with him almost from morning to evening, after he visited his old friend Zi Qing not long ago. Moreover, he included the story of Cook Ding cutting up an ox for Lord Wen-Hui, which he had written before.

After he finished writing, he showed it to Zi Qing who became the first reader of "The Fundamentals for the Cultivation of Life," which opened a new path in health preservation.

The two old men of great attainments in their respective fields talked as they drank. Zi Qing said:

"Master, I'm little educated, but I feel that I can understand all what you write in your articles easily. Compared with the remarks of Confucius and Mo Zi, yours not only have more profound meaning, but also show greater literary grace. They often coincide with the feelings in my heart. The only thing is that I can't express them in words, nor can I write them."

"This precisely means that you understand them tacitly. I can think, write and speak about your flying dragon, but I can't make it," Zhuang

Zhou replied.

"The beginning of this health preservation piece is out of the ordinary: 'There is a limit to our life, but to knowledge there is no limit. With what is limited to pursue what is unlimited is a perilous thing.' This is the truth in life," Zi Qing said after taking a sip of wine. Zhuang Zhou also took a sip and said:

"Brother Zi, it's good wine, just as good as my book!"

Zi Qing read "The Happy Excursion" again and said:

"Brother Zhuang Zhou, It's a good book, just as good as my wine."

The two old friends of great literary skills, who cherished the same ideas, talked as they drank. They talked extensively and did not stop until Lin Qie and Zhuang Yuan took Zhuang Zhou home.

Before Zhuang Zhou left, Zi Qing said:

"Brother Zhuang, when I have good wine, I'll wait for you to drink it!"

Zhuang Zhou turned back and said:

"When I have a good article, I'll ask you to read it!"

On his way back home, Zhuang Zhou said:

"I want to write a piece 'The Human World' at the invitation of Zi Qing to exhort the people that they should know both the role of usefulness and the role of uselessness. Lin Qie, look at the trees in the mountain forests. They are all felled by axes with wooden handles. When the oil burns, it makes itself suffer. Because the cassia bark is eatable, people fell it. As the juice from trees can be used, so people cut them. Man and things each have their own principles."

"Master, point out a bright road for the people, and also put up an alarm bell for some people." Lin Qie understood what was on Zhuang's Zhou's mind.

"Yes."

After returning home, Zhuang Zhou began to write "The Human World." He made use of the words and deeds of Confucius and his disciples as the content in the beginning of his work and expressed them in the form of fables.

Unexpectedly, just when he was quickly finishing this piece, Lin Qie and Zi Ling came and wept as they said: "Our father Zi Qing has passed away!"

"Ah." Zhuang Zhou's writing brush dropped on the white silk, which was immediately stained with the black ink.

Zhuang Zhou looked dull for a while, and asked:

"Why, has my good friend Zi Qing also left?"

"We just learned it. So we have come at once to tell you."

"You go first. I want to accompany my old friend on part of his journey," Zhuang Zhou said with tears in his eyes.

Zhuang Zhou carefully cleaned the flying dragon Zi Qing had given to him, making it spotless. Then, with the support of his son, Zhuang Zhou walked slowly out of his courtyard. He signaled to his son not to support him, and walked staggeringly alone with the flying dragon in his hands to express his condolences and have his last look at Zi Qing.

In the mourning shed, Zhuang Zhou declined all advices from the person officiating at the funeral service and asked Lin Qie to open the coffin lid. He saw his old friend lying quietly in the coffin, neatly dressed, as if he was going to attend a solemn rite. He had never before seen Zi Qing dressed up so seriously or wearing such good clothes. He put the lifelike flying dragon slowly beside Zi Qing, and then sang with tears:

How depressed I am to see my old friend off,
How sad I am to have no one drink with me.
Riding on the flying dragon, you wander about free and
*   unfettered,*
I wonder who else will admire my beautiful articles.

Zhuang Zhou's words and deeds aroused curiosity, discussion and criticism among the watching crowd, mourners and the person who officiated the service.

The person who officiated the service was a scholar. He asked Zhuang Zhou:

"What you've done does not conform to the rule!"

Zhuang Zhou replied:

"What's the rule? The human feelings cannot be feigned. You've ravaged the true feelings of the people and turned the mourning service into a rigid form. Therefore, there are various ways of weeping and crying. Zi Qing is my old friend. No other than I know him well."

As he finished speaking, Zhuang Zhou left staggering, without turning his head.

After he finished three other pieces in a row, Zhuang Zhou felt very lonely. Lin Qie and Zhuang Yuan must carry on their business of making shoes apart from sorting out his manuscripts, leaving not much time for them to talk with him. He felt as if relieved of a heavy load and walked more easily, so he went to see Hui Shi who had been confined to bed paralyzed for a long time. He had only this old friend now. Hui Ze had died long ago. Su Yu, who was not his friend but was on speaking terms, had died of illness long ago.

Zhuang Zhou came to Hui Shi's house. This former prime minister of a state, who was once all-powerful, had already been unvisited, with nobody caring about him. He walked slowly into Hui Shi' house and shouted several times, and Hui Shi who was lying on his bed began groaning. Hui Shi had already been unable to see or to hear others clearly. He was only breathing faintly and painfully.

Zhuang Zhou walked out of Hui Shi's court-yard door, dejected. The scenes when they were childlren and young people appeared again before his eyes.

In a few days, Hui Shi died.

After spending a few lonely years, Zhuang Zhou caught cold by accident, was confined to bed without drinking and eating anything, and gradually lost consciousness. Lin Qie and Zhuang Yuan talked over how to prepare for his funeral affairs, and asked Zi Qing's apprentices to make a coffin for him.

The carpenters' noises awakened Zhuang Zhou. Lin Qie and Zhuang Yuan said happily:

"You've woken up at last!"

"You don't have to make a coffin. After I die, you'll take me to Mt. Mengshan and throw me into any gully as you please. That'll be good enough."

The son and daughter-in-law wept when they heard it. Lin Qie said:

"How can it be like this? Not only Zhuang Yuan and his wife will not agree, but also your disciples and your readers, believers and fellow villagers will not agree either. They want to hold a solemn funeral service for you so as to honour your remarkable contributions and life of frustrations."

Zhuang Zhou signaled to his son to help him sit up. He panted for breaths and said with a sigh:

"Lin Qie, you are not my good disciple. You do not know what's on my mind. After I die, use Heaven and the Earth as my coffin. One may well say it's big enough. Use the sun and the moon as the burial jades. One may well say it's bright and enduring. Use the stars as pearls, one may well say it's precious. Use all things in Heaven and on the Earth as offers for the fasts, one may well say it's a lot. Nature gives you the best and most ideal burials. Who else can match me?"

Lin Qie said:

"We are afraid that if you are thrown on the mountain, crows and sparrow hawks will eat your flesh!"

"If I am thrown on the mountain, you are afraid that crows and sparrow hawks will eat my flesh. If I am buried under the ground, are you not afraid the mole crickets and ants will eat my flesh?"

"This ...." Lin Qie had nothing to say.

The son and daughter-in-law just wept.

Zhuang Zhou gasped for breaths for a while before he said:

"Isn't it clear that you are taking my flesh out of the mouth of the crows and sparrow hawks and giving it to the mole crickets and ants? Are you so partial in dividing my flesh?"

When Zhuang Zhou saw his son and daughter-in-law and Lin Qie become calm, he signaled to them to stop making the coffin. He was gratified and to their surprise, had a small bowl of chicken soup with the help of his daughter-in-law.

He lay on his bed and his thoughts and feelings surged up like clouds and tides. He recalled his father who had died too early, his mother for whom he had boundless respect, his good friend the old fisherman and the horse who knew human feelings, the warm scenes when he visited the State of Chu, Wu Tong's family, scenes of his visits to the states of Wei, Lu and Zhao, Chunyu Kun with superb talent, his good schoolmate Hui Shi, his bosom friend Zi Qing with superb craftsmanship, Lin Qie, his son and daughter-in-law. He could never forget his wife Yan Yu who had always been placed at the bottom of his recollections!

The moonlight shone into the room through the window. Zhuang Zhou moved his head close to the window and saw through a hole the bright moon hanging in the dark blue sky and shedding its bright light all over the earth. He murmured to himself:

"Yan Yu, my good wife, where are you?"

"I'm at the top of Mt. Mengshan!" He clearly heard Yan Yu's reply.

"Well, I'm coming to see you."

Zhuang Zhou suddenly felt much relaxed. So he put on his clothes, left his bed, opened the door, left the house and the courtyard without disturbing his son and daughter-in-law.

The moon hung high like a huge lantern, illuminating the road for Zhuang Zhou. He walked slowly to the graves of his father and mother.

It was the time when spring was dwindling into summer. He gathered a handful of flowers and weeds and a branch of pine twigs, and placed them before the graves. The flowers, weeds and pine twigs put forth a sweet smell of fragrance. Then, he kneeled to kowtow. He rose and went to the grave of Yan Yu, but no matter how he looked for it, he could not find it. He sat on the ground dejected. Suddenly a voice rang in his ears clearly:

"I'm at the top of Mt. Mengshan!"

"Ah, I'm really muddled. Yan Yu is waiting for me at the top of Mt. Mengshan!"

Zhuang Zhou stood up and walked toward the top of Mt. Mengshan.

The next day, Lin Qie and Zhuang Yuan found him disappearing. When the villagers learned that Zhuang Zhou had disappeared, they all went out spontaneously to look for him. They covered all parts of Mt. Mengshan, Mengze Lake and the Menghe River, but found no trace of him. Ten days, two weeks, one month, six months and one year passed, but they never found his trace.

Someone said that Zhuang Zhou had become a butterfly and was dancing in the flowering shrubs.

Another said that Zhuang Zhou had changed into a roc and flown to the distant sea.

Some said that Zhuang Zhou had changed into a flying dragon and flown into the air over the East Sea.

Others said that Zhuang Zhou had turned into colourful clouds and was flying over the top of Mt. Mengshan.

In short, the whereabouts of Zhuang Zhou became an enigma.

It was like this that a bright star fell from the sky. A golden star that will shine forever has risen at Mt. Mengshan.

It was like this that Zhuang Zhou carved two big glittering characters deeply and indelibly on the ancient land of China with his literary talent, courage, insight, speculation, gift, moral quality, as well as his extraordinary experiences, deeds and final settling place — "Zhuang Zi."

It was like this that Zhuang Zhou walked out of Mt. Mengshan and out of China toward the diverse and complicated world. He walked out of the Warring States Period and out of the ancient times toward the infinite future.

图书在版编目（CIP）数据

庄子的故事/张福信著.
—北京：外文出版社，2002.6
ISBN 7-119-03070-1

I.庄… II.张… III.庄周(前 369~前 286) —生平事迹—英文
IV.B223.5

中国版本图书馆 CIP 数据核字（2002）第 039777 号

英文翻译　　章挺权
英文责编　　梁良兴
责任编辑　　吴灿飞　贾先锋
封面设计　　王　志
插图绘制　　李士伋
印刷监制　　冯　浩

外文出版社网址：
　http://www.flp.com.cn
外文出版社电子信箱：
　info@flp.com.cn
　sales@flp.com.cn

庄子的故事

张福信　著

*

©外文出版社
外文出版社出版
（中国北京百万庄大街 24 号）
邮政编码　100037
春雷印刷厂印刷
中国国际图书贸易总公司发行
（中国北京车公庄西路 35 号）
北京邮政信箱第 399 号　邮政编码　100044
2002 年(36 开)第 1 版
2003 年第 1 版第 2 次印刷
（英）
ISBN 7-119-03070-1/I.722(外)
03500(平)
10-E-3488 P